ELEMENTS

STARTING A REVOLUTION IN YOUR WORLD

BY BOB FRANQUIZ
copyright 2005

for carey, the greatest woman i know.

Elements: Starting a revolution in your world

Library of Congress Control Number 2005931677

Fuel Media Group, Inc.
15305 N.W. 60th Ave. Suite 100
Miami Lakes, FL 33014

Edited by Sacha Kauffman
Cover Design by noiz
Interior Design by noiz
Back Cover Photo by Oscar Falero
Printed in the United States of America

elements

THIS BOOK WOULD NOT HAVE BEEN POSSIBLE HAD IT
NOT BEEN FOR THE FOLLOWING PEOPLE:

A GREAT MANY THANKS…

Sacha Kauffman, who edited the mess that was my manuscript!

Deven Christopher, designer extraordinaire, who gave my words an image!

To the congregation that calls Calvary Fellowship home – It is my privilege to be your Pastor and teacher!

To my staff at Calvary Fellowship – You guys are the best!

To my parents, who taught me so many important life lessons that have made me the man I am today…

To the love of my life, Carey – thank you for allowing me to stay up way too late working on this manuscript. Having you at my side makes me the most blessed man on the earth!

And thank you to my Savior, Jesus – I fear to even imagine what my life would be like without You! I'm so glad I never have to, because you will never leave me or forsake me!

ELEMENTS: STARTING A REVOLUTION IN YOUR WORLD

elements

introduction//revolution calling

"You say you want a revolution! Well you know, we all want to change the world…" - The Beatles

I don't know if I believe John Lennon. I don't know if everyone wants to change the world. I would agree that everyone wants change, but not many are willing to pay the price to see that change occur. Most of us usually sit around and play armchair quarterback to all of the problems that befall our world and our lives and say, "Someone should do something about this!" Yet we've never even stopped to consider if that someone is us. Could it be that the reason we see the problem is because God is calling us to be part of the solution and not one of the casualty vampires slowing down to watch the scene of an accident? Most of the people that we deem as heroes, visionaries, and revolutionaries aren't that much different from you or I. They simply just can't stand to watch one more second without doing something. History is full of individuals whose lives we hail as revolutionary. I believe the greatest revolutionaries are found within the pages of the Bible, and I also believe the greatest revolution this planet has ever seen is yet to take place. I sometimes think about what the Apostle Paul alone would have done if he had the computer I am writing these words on, the e-mail program this computer has, and a connection to the Internet. Paul had nothing by our world's standards, and still he was able to accomplish more in half a life than most will accomplish in ten lifetimes. Paul had this innate sense that the time was now and there's not a moment to spare.

But everything exposed by the light becomes visible, for it is light that makes everything

visible. This is why it is said: "Wake up, O sleeper, rise from the dead, and Christ will shine on you." Be very careful, then, how you live—not as unwise but as wise, making the most of every opportunity, because the days are evil. Therefore do not be foolish, but understand what the Lord's will is.

[EPHESIANS 5:13-17 NIV]

Every night of my life, there is this moment just before I fall asleep when I think about the fact that I might not wake up tomorrow. I think that this day may have been my last and, to be honest, sometimes I find that thought frightening. Sometimes it keeps me from falling asleep because I will not go out on that note! I have to make this day worthy of being my last. I grew up watching *Star Trek*, and I have always been a big fan of the Klingons. This warrior race of people don't fear death, instead they embrace it. So when they go into battle they say to one another, "It is a good day to die!" I read an interview with Erwin McManus where he says the same thing to himself each day.[1] For the first time, it made me feel like I wasn't alone in the emotions I was feeling. I can feel the revolution calling me. I sense it like a black hole's gravitational pull draws everything within its reach to itself. It is to this end that God has given me one more day.

When I became a Christian, I didn't walk down an aisle or raise my hand in a church service. My own brother shared the Gospel with me in his kitchen and didn't just tell me about salvation; he spoke to me of discipleship, of denying myself, taking up my cross and following Jesus. I didn't have the wrong impression of the Christian life when I gave my heart to Jesus. In fact, I believe I had a better grip on Christianity than most. Here's what I also know to be true: there is a desire, this inclination to be revolutionary that is in each of us. Some of us bury it, others of us hide from it, still others ignore the call of Jesus to change the world. Yet my greatest fear is that someday I would not hear that still small voice speaking anymore. That is the day I know that I will go to sleep and not wake up the next morning because, truth be told, I will have stopped living long before that.

This book began as a journey for me. I wanted to learn to be a revolutionary Christian, but I found that I had to deal with many obstacles in my own life, including a dual understanding of what a revolution is, to finally be at the place where I am now. Does this mean that my journey is over? Not by a long shot! In fact, I believe that it is only now that my journey is just beginning because one cannot walk the path until he first finds it. So I bid you to come with me on the journey towards greatness. True greatness. Not in the sense that Herod or Alexander were called "Great," but to a higher greatness, a greatness that is bestowed and awarded by none other than Jesus Himself. I believe it is found by retracing the path of one man—the man who started a revolution that we still feel the affects of today. The man whom Jesus called "The greatest man ever born." It is to this man that our journey will lead us, and from this man that our personal journey will embark. My hope is that the elements that comprised his life will become part of our lives through our time with him…

CHAPTER 01

the greatest show on earth

chapter 01//the greatest show on earth

I've heard the word since I was born. I was told how everything
was great until that word entered our lives and our country was
changed from paradise to prison. Please understand. Growing up
in a Cuban family there was really only one topic of conversation to
discuss— Cuba. Everything else was simply a variation of the main
topic, which was always the place my family called home. It didn't
matter what the discussion was:

Food – "IT WAS BETTER IN CUBA."
**"CUBANS REALLY KNEW HOW
TO PLAY BASEBALL."**
Baseball – CUBANS WERE BUILDING
SKYSCRAPERS WHEN
THE REST OF THE
Architecture – THE REST OF THE
WORLD WAS STILL
LIVING IN HUTS."
The beach – LIVING IN HUTS."
**"THE BEACHES IN CUBA WERE
THE ENVY OF THE REST OF THE
WORLD."**

I would get frustrated with this inferred superiority complex. I
remember saying to my parents once, "If Cuba is so great, why don't
you move back there?" At that moment, I knew I had said something
very wrong. As a kid, I was always sticking my foot in my mouth.
But this wasn't the usual slip of the tongue. Everyone in the room
became very quiet. I knew that my parents had moved to America

from Cuba, but at my young age I didn't totally understand why. I had heard the word that summed it all up. I knew the name of the man that led the movement, but I didn't really understand until that day.

A CIVIL WAR OVER REVOLUTION

My family moved to America from Cuba in the mid-1960's in what were called the "Freedom Flights." While many Americans were experimenting with drugs, experiencing Beatle-mania, and taking sides over the Vietnam War, my family was making their exit from the country of their origin to a country 90 miles away that seemed to offer what they had lost—freedom. That is true for many Cuban-Americans who left their homeland to escape "La Revolusion." That's what my family called it— "The Revolution." It was the day Cuba became a Communist country under the regime of Fidel Castro, then a young man. Whenever I hear the word "revolution," I think of that day in my living room when my mom and step-dad told me the story of their beloved Cuba and how in 1959 Fidel Castro and his group of revolutionaries overthrew the government. While they promised a better future for all Cubans, Castro's party eventually allied themselves with the Soviet Union, embraced Marxism, and officially became a Communist country. It was at this time that individual freedoms were taken away one at a time "for the good" of all Cubans. At this point, the handwriting was on the wall: "The Cuba you once loved is gone." But no one expected it to last so long. Most Cubans I have encountered all say that coming to America was only supposed to be for a short time. Many say, "We thought our time in the United States would be five years at the most, and then we could return home." Since I was a child, I have heard stories of people who fled Cuba and the ingenious ways they escaped from their former island paradise to seek freedom. In fact, I was walking out of a popular Cuban restaurant in Miami recently, and on the wall was a framed picture that was featured on the cover of the Miami Herald. It showed several men in a Chevy truck that had been transformed into a raft to make the journey to the shores of America. Many, before they left, buried their life's savings in their backyards, expecting to dig it up once they returned home. It has been over 40 years for some, and they have never had the pleasure of seeing their home and buying a shovel to dig up their earthly treasure.

Yet when I went to school, my teachers would talk of revolution in a positive, triumphant sense. Revolution is what gave us our way of life. Revolution was the backbone of America. I was never much of a student, but the American Revolution has always intrigued me. I grew up in Boston, so being a history buff comes with your first Red Sox cap. Weekends with my dad were filled with history as we visited Plymouth Rock, The U.S.S. Constitution (Old Ironsides), the Old State House, and Bunker Hill. We would walk the Freedom Trail, visit John F. Kennedy's birth home, and climb on board of the reconstructed Mayflower. In Boston, revolution is all around you.

WHAT IS A REVOLUTION?

So as I walk through life as a Cuban-American, I can't help but have mixed feelings about the word "revolution." One part of me stands tall and is proud to have been born in America, which I believe with all my heart is the greatest country ever to grace the pages of history. Yet another part of me thinks of my dad who still gets emotional whenever he sees pictures of his home that he longs to return to. You may be thinking, "So why write a book about revolutionary living? It sounds like you need therapy to get over your issues." While the therapy would probably help me, I've learned something about revolutions. Revolutions refuse to allow the status quo to remain. It's funny because the primary definition of a revolution according to Webster is, "The action by a celestial body of going round in an orbit or elliptical course."[2] To some, a revolution is simply going around in circles. That's where many people live their lives. They are simply going around in circles day in and day out. They do the merry-go-round of wake up, go to work, come home, eat dinner, watch TV, and go to bed. Then they get the pleasure of repeating this series of events for the next 40 years! All the while, there's something inside of them that knows; something that yearns to get off the ride and find true fulfillment and meaning.

The second definition of a revolution according to Webster is, "A sudden, radical, or complete change."[3] The two definitions seem contradictory at first. It could be because a merry-go-round isn't sudden, radical, or completely changing. It is as regular as can be. The earth isn't going to decide at some point to not revolve around the sun. A revolution, we might say, would be for the earth to start moving in figure-8 motions throughout the Milky Way galaxy! But instead, I believe these two ideas can work in tandem with one another.

A REVOLUTION IS A SUDDEN, RADICAL, AND COMPLETE CHANGE.

But I believe that change always revolves around a central idea, person, or belief. In the American Revolution, the idea was that taxation without representation was unacceptable. It revolved around people like Paul Revere, George Washington, and the Continental Congress. The belief was that freedom was worth fighting for, and even dying for. It is the constant revolving around those ideals that has made America the great nation that it is.

EVERYONE IS A REVOLVER

Just like those heroes of old, you also have certain ideas and principles, we might call them "elements," that your life revolves around. You don't realize that's the case because you believe it is just the way you are, but there is something or someone that inspires you to get out of bed in the morning. The day we identify what this is, is the day we will discover what our lives revolve around. What's amazing is that this is very easy to see in others, but much more difficult to see in ourselves. It reminds me of when my wife took me to a sneak preview of the film *Fever Pitch* starring Jimmy

Fallon and Drew Barrymore. This movie is the story of a man whose life is totally consumed by the Boston Red Sox. (My wife wanted to see it because she said she was looking forward to seeing her life on the big screen.) So every decision he made, every appointment, and every relationship simply entered the orbit of his Red Sox universe and all took a backseat to his beloved team. This is where most people live. They live in a world where self is at the center of the universe and God is orbiting our plans, whims, and desires. Yet careful self-evaluation will lead us to discovery in our own lives. We can change the natural revolution of everything circling around us and create a supernatural revolution where we revolve around God and His purposes for redeeming humanity to Himself.

I BELIEVE
EVERY PERSON
WHO PROFESSES JESUS AS
LORD IS CALLED TO BE A
REVOLUTIONARY.

We are called to revolve around the person of Jesus—His words, His life, and His mission. It is by circling this idea that we can create sudden, radical, and complete change! So I considered who could be a model for me in how to live a revolutionary life. How can I be a catalyst for change in my generation? It was then that I started thinking, "If I find this person, he or she will be the greatest person ever to live."

Tom Brokaw made an entire era of people famous with his 1998 book, _The Greatest Generation_. It is here that the courage, sacrifice, and service of the World War II generation is chronicled for all to see and for all, in some way, to give thanks for that generation's contribution to our way of life. I believe that books like these are hard to come by and are fewer and further between than we would like to admit. Unfortunately, bookshelves are filled with cynical works by the Michael Moore's, Jose Canseco's, and Dan Brown's of the world. These books are not raising the bar for man to live, but instead are dragging us down into the mire to be voyeurs and watch the unraveling of politicians, athletes, and institutions. Our challenge is instead to be adventurers, who exist outside of what is considered normal, inspiring others to live great lives.

As I pondered this, I thought once again about Tom Brokaw's greatest generation that was called the greatest in the same way Mohammed Ali was the called the greatest: personal observation (and a knock out or two). Now while I certainly don't disagree with either assumption, I asked myself, "If there's a greatest generation, could there be a greatest man who ever walked the face of the earth?" So I began to search my memory banks to find a man who suited the bill. I am a Christian and a pastor (the first usually has to be true for the second to be true), so my mind immediately went to Jesus. While I could make the argument for Jesus being fully God AND fully man, most would dismiss Him as a candidate for the greatest-man-ever award because of the "fully God" part. So I went further down the list to see if there was a man just like us, without any superpowers, who could fit the bill as the greatest man ever. That's when I thought of him... The perfect candidate with the right credentials and the nomination of the Son of God: John the Baptist. Not David, not Elijah, not Eminem, or Barry Bonds, but John the Baptist. While these other men are greats in their own fields or skill; none had the approval of Jesus Himself as the greatest man ever.

> As John's disciples were leaving, Jesus began to speak to the crowd about John: "What did you go out into the desert to see? A reed swayed by the wind? If not, what did you go out to see? A man dressed in fine clothes? No, those who wear fine clothes are in kings' palaces. Then what did you go out to see? A prophet? Yes, I tell you, and more than a prophet. This is the one about whom it is written: 'I will send my messenger ahead of you, who will prepare your way before you.' I tell you the truth: Among those born of women there has not risen anyone greater than John the Baptist..."

[MATTHEW 11:7-11 NIV]

I've been called the greatest husband ever a few times, the greatest uncle several times; my dad has even called me one of his two favorite sons. (My brother Billy and I have only one another for competition.) But never once have I been called the greatest man ever. Yet as I studied this great man, John the Baptist, here is what I discovered— he doesn't seem all that great. I know that might sound sacrilegious and in opposition to Jesus' teaching. Trust me, it's not. I am simply observing that John the Baptist didn't possess anything that any other person doesn't have.

I wanted the greatest man ever to be someone like Spider-man, so if I was challenged as to why I wasn't more like him I could use exhibit A— "I was not bitten by a radioactive spider, so there's nothing I can do." Then I would pull out exhibit B— "I can't spin webs of any size and catch thieves just like flies." (I've got you singing now.) Then I would bring down the house with exhibit C by letting people know that I don't own a cool red and blue spandex suit (except the Halloween costume when I was eight). At this point, I rest my case and I can go back to living a mediocre, risk free, boring life.

A GREAT DISCOVERY

What I realized is that the greatest man was simply a normal man. He was living out what it meant to follow God in a world that was so vanilla that being any other flavor seemed like "out of the box" living. John the Baptist was a man who didn't play by the rules. He would have been a perfect candidate for "Queer Eye for the Straight Guy" due to the fact that he was such a fashion disaster, and could have done well to watch Emeril's show from time to time to mix up the slop he was eating every day. But all of those things are just symptoms of what was happening on the inside of him that, if we were honest, we would say we want inside of each of us.

Yet most people don't ever experience the level of purpose that John the Baptist felt. While we long for that innately, when we don't achieve it, we naturally don't cheer those on who are living it out daily. Instead, there is something in us that secretly loves seeing people fail, especially those who are famous. I believe it makes some of us feel better about ourselves in some sick way. Their failure gives us reason not to ever try. So we talk about the latest scoop: The newest Hollywood breakup, or which celebrity was photographed without makeup on. I was reading the Boston Globe recently and I got a glimpse of this fact when a headline article featured a celebrity who had purchased an engagement ring for his fiancé (who is also well known), but the diamond wasn't as large as the one he had purchased for his previous fiancé. So I asked myself, "Does anyone care about this?" Then I thought, "I guess, I do. I just read the article!" Just like my reading decisions, we get consumed by the trivialities of life and wonder why we don't achieve greatness. John did achieve greatness, and the reason he did was because he was not consumed by or interested in anything other than being who God created him to be.

In a phrase we could say John the Baptist was a man that lived a life that was consumed by God. That's why he wore what he wore, ate what he ate, and didn't worry about where he slept. Those weren't critical issues to living successfully in the kingdom of God. In fact, Jesus may have had John in mind when he said these words…

> Therefore I tell you, do not worry about your life, what you will eat or drink; or about your body, what you will wear. Is not life more important than food, and the body more important than clothes? Look at the birds of the air; they do not sow or reap or store away in barns, and yet your heavenly Father feeds them. Are you not much more valuable than they? Who of you by worrying can add a single hour to his life? And why do you worry about clothes? See how the lilies of the field grow. They do not labor or spin. Yet I tell you that not even Solomon in all his splendor was dressed like one of these. If that is how God clothes the grass of the field, which is here today and tomorrow is thrown into the fire, will he not much more clothe you, O you of little faith? So do not worry, saying, "What shall we eat?" or "What shall we drink?" or "What shall we wear?" For the pagans run after all these

> things, and your heavenly Father knows that you
> need them. But seek first his kingdom and his
> righteousness, and all these things will be given
> to you as well.
>
> (MATTHEW 6:25-33 NIV)

A REVOLUTIONARY LIFE

What would your life look like if you made God's kingdom your
primary concern? Would your conversations be different? Would
they move beyond box scores, movie reviews, and the weather?
Would they center on issues like why we were put on this planet?
Would your relationships change from functional to influential—
where one encounter with you would change the way people live?
That's what happened to one man who met John. His name was
Apollos and his life was never the same…

> Now a certain Jew named Apollos, born at
> Alexandria, an eloquent man and mighty in the
> Scriptures, came to Ephesus. This man had been
> instructed in the way of the Lord; and being
> fervent in spirit, he spoke and taught accurately
> the things of the Lord, though he knew only the
> baptism of John. So he began to speak boldly in
> the synagogue. When Aquila and Priscilla heard
> him, they took him aside and explained to him
> the way of God more accurately.
>
> (ACTS 18:24-26 NKJV)

Apollos' experience with John changed his entire life. We don't
know what he did prior to meeting John, what his occupation was,
nor what his aspirations were. But once he encountered John, the
entire trajectory of his life was altered so much so, that he missed
out on the whole ministry of Jesus because he had to tell everyone
about his experience with John! I try to imagine what it must have
been like for Pricilla and Aquila listening to this great preacher talk
about John and the need for repentance, and that the Messiah was
coming soon. They must have looked at each other and said, "Won't
he be in for a treat once we give him the punch line to this story!" I
can only imagine what an exciting day it must have been for Apollos.

"So Jesus died?" he says inquisitively.
"Yes, but he rose again," they respond.
"No kidding!" he exclaims.

The church in America has totally missed the boat when it comes to what it means to follow Jesus. We have resolved that to be a follower of Jesus is to repeat a prayer, but neglect living a life to the glory of God. A movement so rich in meaning and purpose that has been watered down to allow us to still go to heaven when we die, but live like hell here on the earth. True Christian faith is an invitation to be part of a revolution. Here is what I also know: you are most likely reading this book because there is something inside of you that longs to know the truth, something that desires to really see things as they are. Perhaps you're a bit like Neo in *The Matrix*, who had this same condition explained to him…

"It's that feeling you have had all your life. That feeling that something was wrong with the world. You don't know what it is but it's there, like a splinter in your mind, driving you mad, driving you to me. But what is it? The Matrix is everywhere; it's all around us, here even in this room. You can see it out your window, or on your television. You feel it when you go to work, or go to church or pay your taxes. It is the world that has been pulled over your eyes to blind you from the truth."

SO THE QUESTION IS, "DO YOU WANT TO KNOW WHAT IT IS?"

The trip is dangerous, the casualties are many, but the result is that you will never be the same. You will be part of an elite group of men and women who decided that "playing church" was not an acceptable way to live; a band of brothers and sisters who believe that the Christian life is the most revolutionary life to be lived because it creates a catalyst of change in our world.

I intentionally left out the last part of verse 11 in Matthew 11. It is here that Jesus gives us the reason He was telling us why John was the greatest man ever.

Assuredly, I say to you, among those born of women there has not risen one greater than John

the Baptist; but he who is least in the kingdom of heaven is greater than he.
(MATTHEW 11:11 NKJV)

Jesus told us all of this about John because you and I have the ability to be greater than John! How is that possible? It is because we are part of the kingdom of God. As a disciple of Jesus, you are among those that are governed by God and desire to see His will done. So it doesn't matter how many times you've failed, how many times you've blown it, how long you've been a follower of Jesus, or how much of the Bible you have memorized. The moment you said, "yes" to Jesus and started walking with Him, none other than God Himself gave to you the potential for greatness! And there is a world that is waiting for you to be consumed by God so they can take notice and get consumed by Him as well…

CHAPTER 02

grand-parents

chapter 02// **grand-parents**

There are so many things that are out of our control. Where we were born, when we were born, and to whom we were born. I was born in 1973 to Ynes and William Franquiz in Boston, Massachusetts. There was no meeting, no memo, not even a choice. I was their son and they were my parents. I remember getting mad at my parents and my dad spinning this tale about how I asked God before I was born if they could be parents and God said, "OK." Even at age eight I knew that wasn't true. That's because there is no way anyone chooses to be born into that kind of dysfunction! I was part of my family against my will and I think others in my family felt the same way. However I sliced it, when I was born, Boston was my home, Nixon was the President, and disco was king. I could have been born anywhere, at any time, to any couple. I think about this probably more than I should. I could have been born in Spain 500 years ago to royalty. In fact, that's where my family tree traces back. At least that's what the guy at EPCOT Center, who sells those family emblems for $200, told me. What I've noticed is that everyone's family is royalty in those records. I guess that helps boost sales. I wouldn't want to buy the family emblem if my ancestors were known as the village idiots. But seriously, I live in the now. I live in the most technologically advanced society ever to inhabit this planet. Yet some days, the only question I can come up with is "why?" Why is it important that I be alive now? I'm sure there were many openings. But I live in the here and now to accomplish something unique to me. The same is true for you. You're not living in Macedonia in 330 B.C. under the rule of Alexander the Great. You're living right now because God decided it in His plan for mankind; this was the best place and time for you to be alive. The Apostle Paul was thinking along these same lines as he spoke of King David…

For when David had served God's purpose in his own generation, he fell asleep; he was buried with his fathers and his body decayed.

(ACTS 13:36 NIV)

There is a reason you are here, a purpose for which you were created. It is here that one's story must begin. To borrow from the runaway best seller, _The Purpose Driven Life_, Rick Warren writes, _"The purpose for your life is far greater than your own personal fulfillment, your peace of mind, or even your happiness. It's far greater than your family, your career, or even your wildest dreams and ambitions. If you want to know why you were placed on this planet, you must begin with God. You were born by His purpose and for His purpose."_[4] If you are going to discover why you were created, the first place to start is with your Creator. Think about what it took for you to be sitting wherever you are reading this book. You may not realize this, but you were born out of a race. This race had some serious competition. There were 50 million contestants and only one winner. What was the prize, you might be wondering? It wasn't a gold medal, or lots of money. It was...an egg. The reason you are here today is because you won the race! So there are statements that we can never make about ourselves. We can never say, "I never win anything!" Or "I'm not a good swimmer!" (If you still don't get this, talk to your wife or your mom.)

THERE IS A REASON YOU ARE WHERE YOU ARE, AND HAVE CERTAIN EXPERIENCES IN YOUR PAST. ALL OF THESE THINGS CULMINATE INTO THE PERSON YOU ARE TODAY.

GREAT EXPECTATIONS

Elizabeth and Zechariah were Jews from the tribe of Levi. They were godly people who had devoted themselves to serving God with all of their lives. Yet in spite of their sincere devotion, God gave them no children. It seemed as though all hope of having a family was lost due to their advancement in years, but what they did not know was that God was waiting. He had prepared for them to give birth and have a part in the spiritual formation of the greatest man ever born. But it had to be when the time was just right. Years past. At just the right time God aligned a series of events, schedules, and even the time of day to deliver the news.

> **In the time of Herod king of Judea there was a priest named Zechariah, who belonged to the priestly division of Abijah; his wife Elizabeth was also a descendant of Aaron. Both of them were upright in the sight of God, observing all the Lord's commandments and regulations blamelessly. But they had no children, because Elizabeth was barren; and they were both well along in years. Once when Zechariah's division was on duty and he was serving as priest before God, he was chosen by lot, according to the custom of the priesthood, to go into the temple of the Lord and burn incense. And when the time for the burning of incense came, all the assembled worshipers were praying outside.**
> (LUKE 1:5-10 NIV)

In the days of the second temple, the number of priests had grown astronomically. Some scholars believe priests numbered over 20,000 in the first century, which meant that not everyone could serve at the same time. This problem had already existed in the days of King David, so in 1 Chronicles 24 he divided the priests into 24 groups. This way every priest could serve, even if it meant on a limited basis. So the priests would serve in the temple two weeks out of the year and then return home until their next scheduled time. Talk about great vacation benefits! Zechariah was in the eighth group— the division of Abijah— and his turn came for service to the Lord in the Temple. Yet while the schedule was decided by calendar, the duties were decided by casting lots. Lots were similar to drawing straws or rolling dice. It was a chance means to fairly choose who would handle certain responsibilities during the priests' tour of duty. God worked it out so that Zechariah would have the privilege of burning incense in the holy place. This was the area where only priests could go that just preceded the Holy of Holies, where God's Presence dwelt. Needless to say, this was a huge honor. As a priest, you could go a lifetime and never have the honor of serving in this great capacity. Because not only was your job to light the incense, which was a symbol of the prayers of God's people rising to heaven, you had the opportunity to pray a very special prayer on behalf of all of God's people. A portion of the prayer was as follows:

"Send us the one who will prepare the way in the desert; the way of the coming of the Lord…"[5]

It was at that moment that God sent an angel to change Zechariah's life forever. Since the temple was built, priests had been reciting that prayer twice a day for 900 years! What are the odds that this day, this time, and this man would be the combination God used? Because at that moment the angel showed up and said, "God is going to answer you now."

I was thinking about this recently while I was watching a Red Sox game on TV. Most of my life has been in the pursuit of one thing: not money, not power, not the Holy Grail— just a baseball. My dream, since I was seven years old and went to my first baseball game at Fenway Park, has been to catch a foul ball at a Major League Baseball game. I know it doesn't seem like a huge dream, but it's what I want! So here's what happened while I was watching the Sox on TV: There was a ball hit foul down the right field line and into the stands when all of a sudden, a fan jumped up, extended his glove, and snagged the ball! It was an amazing catch! Then they closed in on the fan and it was Doug Flutie. Now if you don't know who Doug Flutie is, you definitely aren't from Boston. Doug Flutie is an NFL quarterback today, but on November 23, 1984, he became an immortal when he threw what is simply known today as "The Pass." He led the Boston College Eagles to victory over the Miami Hurricanes in the Orange Bowl with this one "Hail Mary" pass. It is one of the greatest sports moments ever…

WELL, BACK TO THE STORY.

So the announcers decided to interview Doug Flutie for making the catch of the evening. He said the following sentence that drives me out of my mind: "I can't believe it. I've been to four Red Sox games this year and I've caught a foul ball at each game!" I was crushed. That's just not fair. Then I started researching the odds of catching a foul ball at a baseball game. It's close to 1 in 2.5 million. I was not encouraged by this information. So my pursuit continues…

Yet what we don't realize is what the odds were of Zechariah being picked to be pray that prayer on that day. It was easily ten times more unlikely than catching a ball at a baseball game. This can only be attributed to God's sovereign design. The angel, Gabriel, told Zechariah about John's destiny and God's plan for him. Zechariah and Elizabeth knew he would be someone God would use mightily and they brought John up as such. They were great parents because they set John up to succeed. I can only imagine the kind of encouragement and affirmation that these two godly parents gave their young son as he was growing up. Many people look at parenting as something that comes naturally. That's probably because the process of making a baby comes very naturally. But eventually parents get stuck in a rut. Then we start asking the serious questions like, "I don't know what God wants me to do with my kids. What should I do?" I say, "Why don't you assume that God wants to use them! Assume that God has something unique to share with their lives and that your role is to prepare them for their moment to make a difference for the kingdom of God." In fact, we don't have to assume it; God has already told us: *"Teach your children to choose the right path, and when they are older, they will remain upon it" (Proverbs 22:6 NLT).* Zechariah and Elizabeth had an understanding that God makes the man, but parents shape the man. That's why the story ends as beautifully as it begins...

> When it was time for Elizabeth to have her baby, she gave birth to a son. Her neighbors and relatives heard that the Lord had shown her great mercy, and they shared her joy. On the eighth day they came to circumcise the child, and they were going to name him after his father Zechariah, but his mother spoke up and said, "No! He is to be called John." They said to her, "There is no one among your relatives who has that name." Then they made signs to his father, to find out what he would like to name the child. He asked for a writing tablet, and to everyone's astonishment he wrote, "His name is John..." The neighbors were all filled with awe, and throughout the hill country of Judea people were talking about all these things. Everyone who heard this wondered about it, asking, "What then is this child going to be?" For the Lord's hand was with him... And the child grew and became strong in spirit; and he lived in the desert until he appeared publicly to Israel."
> (LUKE 1:57-66; 80 NIV)

PARENTAL GUIDANCE REQUIRED

Have you ever seen the ESPN Strong Man competition? That's just great TV. Guys lifting weights is fine, but let's get these guys chopping wood or ripping a tire with their bare hands. That's real strength! Yet real inner strength comes from God and is nurtured by loving parents. It's not everyday that a brand new set of parents have a hand in shaping the life of the greatest man ever.

So here's the question to ask yourself to see if you're shaping a great man or woman: *"Am I encouraging him/ her to make God the most important Person in his/ her life?"* I know most of us want that to be the case, but are we actively encouraging the children under our care to vigorously pursue a passionate relationship with God? Parenting is about teaching children that God's way is best even if they don't understand it because there will be a day when you aren't there to make the choice for them. Too many kids follow God only until they leave for college. Once they experience the freedom of being on their own, that's when we find out if their relationship with God was theirs or simply an extension of their parents'. That's why Proverbs 22:6 says even when they get older and have the choice, they will remain on God's path. If you look at your parental role as primarily a molder and shaper, someday your kids will make the right decisions on their own without your help. The kids in our youth group amaze me. They are passionate young adults that want to walk with God. I hear great stories of how they say "no" to parties or extra-curricular activities at school if it will interfere with their involvement at our Friday night youth meetings. That's not to say that this is all their relationship with God entails. It simply means that this is the tip of the iceberg. But a great deal of these students are watching this attitude being modeled by parents that see themselves as spiritual stimulators in their lives.

The human condition is so interesting because to get the result we want, we have to model it. Simply talking about it won't do. I talk to parents who are having problems with their children and they ask me what book they should read to help them with rebellious kids. I tell them, "I would get a book on felonies and misdemeanors. That way when the police

PARENTING IS ABOUT TEACHING CHILDREN THAT GOD'S WAY IS BEST EVEN IF THEY DON'T UNDERSTAND IT BECAUSE THERE WILL BE A DAY WHEN YOU AREN'T THERE TO MAKE THE CHOICE FOR THEM.

officer shows up, you will understand the terms he's using!" Most of the time we want to make a drastic change, but it's a little too late.

THEY WILL NOT MAKE GOD THE MOST IMPORTANT PERSON IN THEIR LIVES IF HE IS NOT THE MOST IMPORTANT PERSON IN YOUR LIFE.

What I have observed from great parents is that their parenting was the result of having a plan and then following through consistently. Amazingly, there are not that many verses in the Bible that deal directly with parenting. There are principles, stories, and inferences we can make, but as far as "Parents should do this…" verses, they are few and far between. I think that's because God wants our focus not to be on the technique of parenting in the sense of, "Should I demand feed or put her on a schedule?" or "What does the Bible say his curfew should be?" But our focus should be on molding these young lives into radical disciples of Jesus. What time they are allowed to come home on Friday night is up to you.

PLAN YOUR WORK AND WORK YOUR PLAN

I hear parents say, "Well, my parents didn't have a plan and I turned out OK." Are you sure about that? Or are the pages of your life filled with paragraph after paragraph of regret that you hope your kids never have to repeat? I have a good friend who says he is going to raise his children totally differently than his parents raised him because he's not impressed with the end product his parents produced! My parents are nice people, but they weren't Christians when I was growing up so they never taught me how to walk with God and I made so many mistakes and have regrets because of it. Do I blame them? Of course not. My mistakes are my mistakes, not theirs. No one forced me to jump out of the window of my 9th grade science class. I chose on my own to turn off the power at a classmate's house and to padlock the box so they would have to call a locksmith or use a hacksaw at 4AM. These genius plans were all mine. (My friends Keith and Alan had the power box idea.) But the greatest tragedy is when Christians don't teach their kids to walk with God.

What I have learned is that it's not because parents don't want their children to have a real experience with God; it's just because they are lazy parents. Great parenting is the result of recognizing your role as the shaper in those lives and then giving those under your care the opportunity to become great in God's sight. This doesn't mean you try to control their every move or give them everything they want. Neither extreme is beneficial. It's teaching them how to walk the path even when you aren't there to show the way. It's about showing them how to make God the most important person in their lives. How you do that is up to you. God has entrusted them to you, but I would ask that you look to those who have great kids and ask them. Read everything you can on the subject and become a parenting expert. When I asked Carey to marry me, the first thing I did was get every teaching I could on marriage. I started reading books on marriage and talking to people with great marriages. Why would I do that? It's because I had never seen a good marriage. Both of my parents have been divorced more than once and I never wanted that to be me. So why take the risk with your kids? Be the best parent you can be and reap the rewards of seeing part of your purpose on this earth fulfilled as you train the next generation of people who will walk on God's path.

God probably isn't going to show up in your bedroom and plan out your children's futures. But the fact that they are here tells you that God wants to do something great with them.

MY QUESTION FOR YOU IS,
"ARE YOU
PREPARING
THEM
FOR GREATNESS?"

Have you told them they have great potential? Most people go through their entire lives and are never told that they have the potential for greatness. Whenever I have spoken on this subject at my church or anywhere else for that matter, I have received numerous letters, voice messages, and e-mails from people that were moved by the fact that I told them that they have the potential to be great and make a great impact for the kingdom of God. Growing up I wasn't encouraged in that way. But then I became a Christian and I learned about what God thought of me, and it changed my life forever. He doesn't say things like, "You were a mistake" or "You'll never amount to anything." Some of you have walked through your whole lives without knowing the thoughts that God thinks towards you. There have been other words that were spoken— harmful words, cutting words, hurtful words, and many of you have walked through your lives with a hole needing to be filled with hopeful words. Maybe it has driven you to do things you regret and to have memories that you can't erase. But that can change. You can listen to what God thinks of you. You can hear the words of hope and peace that He wants to shape your life with. You can receive the love that God is sending in your direction and let that shape who you are. Wouldn't that be grand?

> **For I know the thoughts that I think toward you, says the LORD, thoughts of peace and not of evil, to give you a future and a hope.**
> (JEREMIAH 29:11 NKJV)

CHAPTER 03

born to be wild

chapter 03//**born to be wild**

Christmas at the Franquiz household is like Willy Wonka's chocolate factory for every assorted treat. There's cake, candy canes, and cookies galore. Because my wife is an amazing chef, we've spent lots of money investing into her culinary gifts (and my waistline is proof). Yet as much as I love her sugar cookies, there's something that rubs me the wrong way. It's not the taste; it's their size and shape. They're all the same. Every Christmas tree is exactly alike; every angel is the same size; every snowman is perfectly identical. The reason: my wife uses a cookie cutter to expedite the cookie making process. While that is an efficient way to make cookies, it is not for making Christians.

We live in a cookie cutter world. From the time we enter elementary school, we are being hammered with the idea that individuality is not something to strive for. I remember when I was in the seventh grade that the Catholic school I attended had a dress code. Code called for a white shirt, green tie, and green pants. Everyone in the school bought the same type of shirt and the same style of pants. Ties were purchased through the school secretary. Every kid wore green corduroys and a button down white shirt. Aside from the color, no one told them those pants were what needed to be worn, but sure enough everyone went the cookie cutter route and bought what everyone else was wearing. But I wanted to still be an individual in the midst of sameness. I decided corduroys were for idiots when Levi's had Button Fly 501's in green. It seemed like a no-brainer to wear a cool pair of jeans over lame cords. Also, I didn't buy the white shirt everyone else was wearing; I bought a white Polo shirt and slapped the tie on top of that. As you imagine that picture, you may think I looked foolish but believe it or not, by halfway through the school year over 50% of the boys in my class were wearing them.

ONE SIZE FITS ALL?

Unfortunately, the cookie cutter mentality doesn't leave us at graduation. It grows and mutates like a virus to our originality.

MOST PEOPLE SPEND THEIR LIVES TRYING TO BE LIKE OTHERS AS OPPOSED TO THE PEOPLE GOD CREATED THEM TO BE.

That's why we live in cookie cutter homes and wear one size fits all t-shirts. Has there ever been a more radical picture of conformity than "one size fits all" gear? Wherever you are reading this book, stop and take a good look around. Since God has created people of all shapes and sizes, are you under the impression that there is a t-shirt that will fit everyone well? Of course not! Then why make them? Could it be because our society is pushing us towards conformity? While culture finds it vogue to preach uniqueness, it's not something that's rewarded. Those that are different are usually singled out and ostracized. It's not even something people do consciously. I don't believe people are that malicious. It's just that we've never left the schoolyard mentality; the place where the "different" kid usually ate lunch alone.

That's why there's a war going on inside each of us. There is the desire to be unique as God created us to be, while at the same time the desire to belong pulls at us like the words: "All You Can Eat" pull many a man's car into the parking lot of a buffet. It's this tension that Mr. Keating wanted to teach his students. In one of the most insightful scenes in the movie *Dead Poets Society*, Robin Williams' character holds class outside where he wants to teach a group of young men about the tension we are discussing. He asks a few of the students to take a walk around the courtyard. As they do, they begin walking at their own pace, but soon they are all marching in complete unison. At that moment, Mr. Keating stops his experiment and teaches these boys an important lesson…

"Now, I didn't bring them up here to ridicule them. I brought them up here to illustrate the point of conformity: the difficulty in maintaining your own beliefs in the face of others. Now, those of you— I see the look in your eyes like, 'I would've walked differently.' Well, ask yourselves why you were clapping. Now, we all have a great need for acceptance. But you must trust that your beliefs are unique, your own, even though others may think them odd or unpopular, even though the herd may go, 'That's baaaaad.' Robert Frost said, 'Two roads diverged in a wood and I, I took the one less traveled by, and that has made all the difference.' Now, I want you to find your own walk right now. Your own way of striding, pacing. Any direction. Anything you want. Whether it's proud, whether it's silly, anything. Gentlemen, the courtyard is yours."

That's the heart that we see in the man who was the greatest according to Jesus. John the Baptist had a walk that was all his own. Yet it was a walk that we can certainly glean many insights from. Just looking at John would have given you the creeps. He was the kind of guy that you would have avoided at the mall because his look was so radical. Instead, the opposite happened. Multitudes from all around came to see him. Yet it wasn't the "come see the bearded lady" type of seeing. We should say they came from all over "seeking" him. Why? Because a life consumed by God is attractive to others.

In those days John the Baptist came, preaching in the Desert of Judea and saying, "Repent, for the kingdom of heaven is near." This is he who was spoken of through the prophet Isaiah: "A voice of one calling in the desert, 'Prepare the way for the Lord, make straight paths for him.' " John's clothes were made of camel's hair, and he had a leather belt around his waist. His food was locusts and wild honey. People went out to him from Jerusalem and all Judea and the whole region of the Jordan. Confessing their sins, they were baptized by him in the Jordan River.
(MATTHEW 3:1-6 NIV)

Why is that important to us as Christians? Why should some guy dressing like a weirdo influence us? Some of us might have flashbacks of the Rainbow guy waving his John 3:16 flag at every sporting event in the universe. More than what John the Baptist's style of dress said when it came to fashion, his appearance spoke of his relationship with God. The Eastern world is so different than the West when it comes to exchanging ideas and information. In the West, we think in facts and figures. We train children and young adults to be able to recite back to us the information we instill in them. In the East, learning was done in pictures and symbols. Have you ever wondered why God called His prophets to do things we would call "weird?" I read Ezekiel and I just feel bad for the guy. He always got stuck illustrating bad news for the people of Judah. To prove how Israel would be taken into captivity where they would be forced to eat defiled foods, he had to cook his food over manure. Forgive me, but that's just nasty! Let's be honest, if Ezekiel had any friends left after this culinary stunt, I'm sure they wanted to have him fitted for a white jacket with extra long sleeves. But that's the way the Eastern mind works. It sees truth as a picture. That's why John's attire was so important. When people saw him they thought of God. Why? Because the picture of John should have reminded them of another wild prophet they revered…Elijah.

> The king asked them, "What kind of man was it who came to meet you and told you this?" They replied, "He was a man with a garment of hair

Inside every believer is a person who wants to express himself or
herself for God's glory. I want to give you a news flash: God doesn't
use a cookie cutter in His human design. In fact, He doesn't even
own one. The saying, "When they made you, they broke the mold," is
true of every person. Yet the cares of life beat the wildness we were
born with out of us until there's nothing left. And once the wild
desire to uniquely express ourselves has been completely expunged,
the unique message we have been called to share leaves as well.

A MESSAGE FOR YOU

The thing that's amazing about John is that multitudes came to
hear him. His message was clear, simple, and totally relevant to
the culture of his day. *"Repent! For the kingdom of heaven is near!"*
(Matthew 3:2 NIV) Why was this message so cutting edge? Because
no one had talked like that for 400 years! Scholars call them the
silent years. It's the time period from when the Old Testament was
completed to the day before John began his ministry.

We live in a world where we have Christian radio, television, books,
tapes, CDs, Mp3s, bumper stickers, t-shirts, and combs. I've even
seen Christian toenail clippers! We are so inundated with the Gospel
message that we can become hardened to it if we aren't careful. But
in John's day, God was very silent. It was like the calm before the
storm. It could be compared to the days of Eli, the priest of the Lord,
of which it was said…

> **The boy Samuel ministered before the LORD
> under Eli. In those days the word of the LORD
> was rare; there were not many visions.**
> (1 SAMUEL 3:1 NIV)

John came on the scene and started preaching that the kingdom of
God was at hand. In our day we would say, "God's kingdom is just
around the corner, so everyone better get ready!"

The reason God desires for us to live out our God-given originality is so we can share our unique message. God knows the impact of the principle we see in the life of John the Baptist; that a life consumed by God will be attractive to others. Think about all the infomercials we watch. All we see are the testimonies of people who have become consumed with a product. They have experienced firsthand the rewards of their decision to purchase it. It's the reason why marketing people say the best advertisement is a satisfied customer. That's why I tell the congregation I pastor that if they are going to play games with God, and not do what He says, not to call themselves Christians. The reason is because a lukewarm Christian is not going to help the cause of the kingdom of God at all. In fact, they will hinder the cause of Christ. When a young preacher asked D.L. Moody how he could get many people to come hear him preach, Moody responded, "Get on fire for God, and people will show up to watch you burn." What does fire do? It consumes. It shouldn't surprise us that the Bible says, *"For our 'God is a consuming fire'" (Hebrews 12:29 NIV).* What happens to a person who yields himself to God's plan? God consumes him and the fire warms others.

ONE OF A KIND

So I guess the question we need to answer is, "Do I want to be attractive to others so I can reach them with the Gospel?" If I do, then I need to embrace my uniqueness and celebrate it. Whatever my distinctness is, when I leverage that for God's glory the world is attracted to it and the message we are called to share is heard. Yet we have reduced the reason God created us, and the goal of the Christian life to many things. Unfortunately, none of them are what God truly intended. John Eldredge said it best when he wrote…

"Christianity, as it currently exists, has done some terrible things to men. When all is said and done, I think most men in the church believe that God put them on the earth to be a good boy. The problem with men, we are told, is that they don't know how to keep their promises, be spiritual leaders, talk to their wives, or raise their children. But, if they will try real hard they can reach the lofty summit of becoming … a nice guy. That's what we hold up as models of Christian maturity: Really Nice Guys. We

don't smoke, drink, or swear; that's what makes us men. Now let me ask my male readers: In all your boyhood dreams growing up, did you ever dream of becoming a Nice Guy? (Ladies, was the Prince of your dreams dashing . . . or merely nice?) Really now–do I overstate my case? Walk into most churches in America, have a look around, and ask yourself this question: What is a Christian man? Don't listen to what is said, look at what you find there. There is no doubt about it. You'd have to admit a Christian man is . . . bored." [6]

Why should any Christian man or woman be bored? We have the most important message in the world to share and the freedom to express it in a way that's in line with how God created us. So why are we bored? It's because we've removed the wildness and uniqueness out of the Christian life and replaced it with a list of rules to follow. That's not a relationship, that's the directions to a board (pun intended) game. Relationships are unique. They are unpredictable. They are intimate. They are anything but boring.

My wife and I have been married for eight years. On a recent vacation we were having dinner and we couldn't stop talking about what God was doing in our lives. As we were driving home, I turned to her and said, "I'm so glad we don't have the kind of marriage where at dinner we just stare at each other because we have nothing to say." When a relationship has reached the point where there's nothing to say, it's because there isn't much of a relationship anymore. Some say, "Well, we just know each other, that's why there's nothing to say." I disagree. I believe that when there's nothing to talk about and boredom has set in, we have moved from relationship to function. I believe that's why married men and women have extramarital affairs. I don't believe the primary issue is sex.

I BELIEVE THERE'S A DEEPER NEED FOR RELATIONSHIP THAT'S BEEN LOST.

That's why Christians are having spiritual affairs and giving their allegiances to causes that don't compare to the glory of the Great Commission. I've watched men give the best years of their lives to their careers, only to find that it doesn't pay off in the end. Some women will live vicariously through soap operas or romance novels simply to be whisked away from the mundane duties of life. John the Baptist was many things—bored was not one of them. God consumed his life and that attracted others to him.

Whether the adage is true that "nice guys finish last" can be left to the armchair quarterbacks to decide. But this much is certain: nice guys certainly don't get noticed when they've been fit into a preconceived mold. So I want to ask you to do something crazy. It's something you've wished for, but never thought possible. I want you to think about your life without boundaries.

PEOPLE USE THE PHRASE,
"THINKING OUTSIDE THE BOX."
I WANT YOU TO THINK WITH
THIS IN MIND,
"WHERE'S
THE
BOX
EVERYONE
IS TALKING ABOUT?"
THINK ABOUT HOW GOD HAS
UNIQUELY CREATED AND GIFTED
YOU. THEN, IMAGINE A LIFE
WHERE YOU COULD SPEND EVERY
WAKING MOMENT EXPRESSING
YOURSELF IN A WAY THAT LEADS
OTHERS CLOSER TO JESUS.

When I became a follower of Jesus in 1993 two men baptized me in my church. One of them was named Mike Rozell. He was a godly man who had a high paying job and everything that comes with working for a Wall Street firm. Yet despite his successful career he was unhappy. On the outside, we all would have said that Mike was a great Christian guy who served at his church and loved God. When his pastor asked him what he loved to do he responded, "I love to do pottery!" The pastor thought to himself, "Good luck paying your mortgage making coffee mugs and ashtrays!"

Before long, Mike and his wife, Pam, began an experiment called Potter's Field Ministry. This couple travels the country and the world sharing the life-changing message of Jesus as they explain it through Pam's singing and Mike's pottery; they preach that we are all God's workmanship (Ephesians 2:10). Through this ministry thousands have come to faith in Jesus Christ all because one man decided to rediscover his uniqueness and break out of the cookie cutter mold. The result is a life that is consumed by God that's attracting many others to Him as well.

Why live a cookie cutter existence when you could be living an adventure? Think about the life you've always dreamed of… A life that is full of purpose and meaning. What is stopping you from seizing it? If you don't you will wake up years from now and wonder what happened to all the time. There were so many things you wanted to do for God but never got around to it. Please understand, I have sat with people on their deathbeds and had them tell me with tears in their eyes that they missed it; that they lived in the mold someone else set out for them. They followed the rabbit trail of "Make lots of money, get a big house, and be the envy of the neighborhood." Yet inside they were dying! That doesn't have to ever be said of a follower of Jesus because we can seize the day and make a difference that lasts for eternity. I wonder what Mr. Keating would say to us…

"'Gather ye rosebuds while ye may.' The Latin term for that sentiment is Carpe Diem. Now who knows what that means?"

"Carpe Diem. That's 'seize the day.'"

"Very good, Mr.-"

"Meeks."

"Meeks. Another unusual name. Seize the day. Gather ye rosebuds while ye may. Why does the writer use these lines?"

"Because he's in a hurry."

"No, ding! Thank you for playing anyway. Because we are food for worms lads. Because, believe it or not, each and every one of us in this room is one day going to stop breathing, turn cold, and die. Now I would like you to step forward over here and peruse some of the faces from the past. You've walked past them many times. I don't think you've really looked at them. They're not that different from you, are they? Same haircuts. Full of hormones, just like you. Invincible, just like you feel. The world is their oyster. They believe they're destined for great things, just like many of you. Their eyes are full of hope, just like you. Did they wait until it was too late to make from their lives even one iota of what they were capable? Because you see gentlemen, these boys are now fertilizing daffodils. But if you listen real close, you can hear them whisper their legacy to you. Go on, lean in…Carpe. Hear it? Carpe. Carpe Diem. Seize the day boys, make your lives extraordinary…."

CHAPTER 04

snowplow

chapter 04//**snowplow**

I never played a game of football in high school for two reasons: #1, I didn't have at least a 1.5 GPA that would have made me eligible to play, and #2, I didn't want to play the position they had for me. During practice, I was playing defensive tackle. I liked that position. I got to hit people and sack quarterbacks! Then one day, the coach decided that I might be better as an offensive lineman. I agreed to give it a try and it was terrible! I never got to touch the football. My coach just said, "Franquiz, you're strong. We need you to create openings for the running backs to get yards." Let me translate that for you: "Franquiz, you're fat. Just use your enormous mass to open a hole for the good players to score, so by the time you get to the end zone, the celebration will be over!" So I quit and my high school football career was over! Unfortunately, the extra free time didn't help my grades.

We all want to be the person who scores the touchdown, hits the walk-off home run, or makes the final shot at the buzzer. In a phrase, we want to be the main event. Some try to deny it or hide, but let's face it, we love being the center of attention. Back in the band I was in, arguments would always arise over which band would be the opening act and which band would "headline" the show. Why such "intense fellowship" even amongst Christian band members? It is because no one wants to be the opening act. Once we were playing a show in Tampa and we were talking it over with the other band as to who was going to play first. We didn't want to play first and neither did they, but since they had come from San Diego, we gave in and let P.O.D. play after us! Years later, he's on MTV Cribs and I am sitting at home. I didn't have a problem seeing one friend on MTV Cribs, but when I saw two other friends that are in different bands, it started to bug me a little. No one prepares all of his or her life to be an opening act. Well, one man did but he was the greatest man ever.

He was the guy with the elements to start a revolution in his world, and if we implement those elements into our lives we can start a revolution in ours as well.

PLOWING AWAY

What was John the Baptist's role? He was just a snowplow. Growing up in Boston has a few certainties attached to it: learning a great deal about the founding of America, having your heart broken by the Red Sox year after year (prior to October 27th, 2004 when the Red Sox won it all and I think the world stopped turning), and, of course, snow. I don't mean just enough snow to cover everything to make it a white Christmas. I mean snow that stops traffic, cancels school, and is rolled into the bodies of a 1,000 snowmen. Snow is a reality in Boston that no one can escape. Yet the ever-ingenious Bostonian has learned the art of living in these arctic conditions—the art of the snowplow. The snowplow attaches to the front of some four-wheel drive "man's man" pick-up truck and pushes its powdery villain to the front of everyone's lawns so that the roads will be clear. Right behind him is someone adding salt to the roads to melt the ice. This is the recipe to rescuing a city full of people from being trapped in their homes.

As important as having a snowplow is in the world of winter, there is need for spiritual snowplows that will cut through all the religious fluff to show us the right way to God. That was the job description of the world's greatest man. He wasn't the main event. He was the opening act. John was simply that—a snowplow clearing the way for Jesus to show up on the scene. Many of us miss out on God's best for our lives because we feel we have to be the main event.

WHEN I DECIDE THAT MY OBJECTIVE IN LIFE IS TO BE THE CENTER OF ATTENTION, I AM LIKE A PARKED CAR IN THE MIDDLE OF THE STREET. I AM NOT CLEARING THE PATH FOR PEOPLE TO GET TO GOD; INSTEAD, I AM OBSTRUCTING THE PATH.

Being in the spotlight is not the goal of life. The goal for us as Christians should be to become the people God has created us to be. That's where success is found for each of us. But it takes something to accept the role God has for you—humility. In our day and age, to be called humble is like someone insulting your mom; it's rude! I believe this is because we have a wrong perspective as to what humility is. Here is my definition, "Humility is knowing who I am in light of who God is." John had it and that's what made him great, and I believe if we add it to our lives, it has the potential to make us great as well.

"KNOW YOUR ROLE!"

But part of growing as a Christian and engaging in revolutionary living is to follow the advice of pro wrestler turned actor, The Rock. He told audiences, "The Rock says, 'Know your role.'" That's great advice, even if it comes from "The most electrifying man in sports entertainment!" If you are going to be a catalyst for change in this world, you need to know your role. Why has God placed you on this planet? Best selling author Rick Warren wrote in his book, _The Purpose Driven Life_,

"If you want to know why you were placed on this planet, you must begin with God. You were born by his purpose and for his purpose. The search for the purpose of life has puzzled people for thousands of years. That's because we typically begin at the wrong starting point—ourselves. We ask self-centered questions like 'What do I want to be?' 'What should I do with my life?' 'What are my goals, my ambitions, my dreams for my future?' But focusing on *ourselves will never reveal our life's purpose...You didn't create yourself, so there is no way you can tell yourself what you were created for!"[7]*

As a pastor, the question I hear the most is, "What's God's will for my life?" Instead, we should be asking the question that John Eldredge's pint size powder keg of a book *Epic* asks us to consider: "What is the story God is telling and what is my role to play?"[8] The problem is, we live in a world where we are taught from birth that "second" is a bad word. Someone once asked the famous conductor Leonard Bernstein, "What is the hardest position to fill in an orchestra?" He said, "Second Chair." It shouldn't surprise us. It's ingrained into us from the time we're born that everything is about being number one. When was the last time you spoke with a child who told you his dream was to be Vice President of the United States? I have never had anyone tell me that. I have had many say, "President." The reason is because no one wants to take the backseat and be second. No young dreamer is longing to be a co-star in a movie. They want to be THE star. In fact, the movie "Indiana Jones and the Last Crusade" almost had someone other than Sean Connery playing Professor Jones. The reason? The former 007 wanted to be the top billing. That's outrageous! He wasn't even Indiana Jones and he still wanted to be first. Similarly, many people miss out altogether on God's best because they have to be first. That wasn't the way of the greatest man. John the Baptist's life is one that screams through the pages of history that happiness is found when we know our roles.

> After these things Jesus and His disciples came into the land of Judea, and there He remained with them and baptized. Now John also was baptizing in Aenon near Salim, because there was much water there. And they came and were baptized. For John had not yet been thrown into prison. Then there arose a dispute between some of John's disciples and the Jews about purification. And they came to John and said to him, "Rabbi, He who was with you beyond the Jordan, to whom you have testified—behold, He is baptizing, and all are coming to Him!" John answered and said, "A man can receive nothing

unless it has been given to him from heaven. You yourselves bear me witness, that I said, 'I am not the Christ,' but, 'I have been sent before Him.' He who has the bride is the bridegroom; but the friend of the bridegroom, who stands and hears him, rejoices greatly because of the bridegroom's voice. Therefore this joy of mine is fulfilled. He must increase, but I must decrease."

(JOHN 3:22-30 NKJV)

John the Baptist found happiness, purpose, and fulfillment when he took on the role of the spiritual snowplow. People were pressuring him to take on a bigger role, to assume a place of importance, but he refused. He was content to be who God had created him to be and to fulfill the role that God had uniquely gifted him for.

Now this was John's testimony when the Jews of Jerusalem sent priests and Levites to ask him who he was. He did not fail to confess, but confessed freely, "I am not the Christ." They asked him, "Then who are you? Are you Elijah?" He said, "I am not." "Are you the Prophet?" He answered, "No." Finally they said, "Who are you? Give us an answer to take back to those who sent us. What do you say about yourself?" John replied in the words of Isaiah the prophet, "I am the voice of one calling in the desert, 'Make straight the way for the Lord.'"

(JOHN 1:19-23 NIV)

HUMBLE PIE

I believe the first ingredient for any person that aspires to be great is humility. This is simply recognizing who we are in light of who God is. Too many times Christians try to wear humility like a hat and it turns out to be a false humility. That's why it drives me crazy when I hear pastors say, "I have no idea what I'm doing running this church." If that were true, someone who loved you would have thrown you out long ago. But instead if you're a good leader, admit it. I believe my strongest spiritual gift is teaching, thus I believe I am a good Bible teacher. Please note, I didn't say great, or marvelous, nor did I compare myself to the great saint of old, John Chysostom, who was nicknamed "golden throat." But to say you are good at something because God has given you a gift isn't pride; it is simply good stewardship. Now if I were to tell you that I was an amazing handyman, it wouldn't be false humility; it would just be a lie! That's why Paul told us…

> As your spiritual teacher I give this piece
> of advice to each one of you. Don't cherish
> exaggerated ideas of yourself or your
> importance, but try to have a sane estimate of
> your capabilities by the light of the faith that
> God has given to you all.
>
> (ROMANS 12:3 JBP)

I find most people don't have a sober view of themselves and it creates problems for them in life. Imagine a scale. In the middle is humility—knowing who I am in light of who God is. On right is the inflated view of self where I'm not seeing myself IN light of who God is; instead, I see myself by MAKING light of who God is. That's called pride. Carey and I have similar computers and hers has this sound it makes from time to time. I asked about the sound and she said, "It makes that noise when I make a mistake. Do you have it?" I said, "Probably, we have the same computer." My next thought was, "If I don't hear it, it must mean I don't make any mistakes." I hadn't even said anything when Carey replied, "That doesn't mean you don't make mistakes, it just means you don't have the sound turned on." That's pride—thinking higher of yourself than you ought.

We can slip to the other extreme where we don't think we are good at anything, and dishonor the gifts God has entrusted us with. What if I bought you a new Ford Mustang? Obviously, we are playing make believe. I think we could both agree that a new Mustang is a nice gift. Do you think it would honor me as the giver of the gift if every time you took your friends out in the car you talked about what a piece of junk it was? No way! In fact, if you did that, I would take that car back and give you a bus pass! So let's not do that with the gifts God has given us or in the roles God has placed us in.

John's acceptance of his role as God's snowplow flies in the face of every cultural instinct we are supposed to have. Yet John was able to rise above the cultural hype and function in the role that God had for him from the foundations of the earth. Think about it: John's role was talked about 750 years before John was even born. Talk about job security!

YET MOST OF US WOULD ASPIRE TO BE MORE. NOT THAT THE KINGDOM OF GOD MIGHT BE FURTHERED, BUT SO THAT OUR NAMES MIGHT BE KNOWN.

Most of us go through life like George Costanza from "Seinfeld." In an episode called "The Salad," George buys Elaine a salad, but it is George's new girlfriend who gives it to her. Elaine thanks the new girlfriend, but George will have none of that. So George decides that it is better to have people know who bought the salad and risk losing a relationship. So what happened? The same thing that always happens. George gets dumped for being an idiot! I wonder if we have gone Costanza-like in life—seeking for everyone to know who we are as opposed to who Jesus is. John's character and focus on what was most important became the key ingredients to his greatness.

We forget that John's dad was Zechariah, a priest in the Temple of God. As the son of a priest, John's rite was to follow in his dad's footsteps and take on the prestigious role of being a priest in the house of God. I'm sure the position came with full benefits and dental! But John chose rather to walk away from that life and serve God in a special capacity. This type of person is hard to come by. There have been some who have inked the pages of Scripture and some who have walked with us that have made us better people by being John-like Christians. I think of my friend John who was successful in the computer field. He and his wife, Tania, a nurse, sold everything they owned to serve the Muslim community in the Middle East. My friend Paul left an opportunity to double his salary at his company to teach pastors in the slums of Nairobi, Kenya. These people aren't superstars. They simply live in a world where most of us have made being comfortable the supreme goal of our lives. That's why a man like John the Baptist amazes us so much. He's so real it makes everything around him look fake.

WASSUP DOG?

The basis for all service is humility. If our goal is to reflect God in all aspects of our lives then humility is not only necessary, but also vital. Think about the Incarnation for a moment. We don't see it as a big deal to become human because that's what we are. But God, who created the heavens and the earth and encompasses time and space, crammed Himself into a body. To make matters worse, Jesus didn't just become human. He was born as a baby. To add a little more insult to injury, He was born to a poor family in a seemingly insignificant city. How small was "O Little Town of Bethlehem?" Imagine all the babies under two years old being killed by a king (Matthew 2) and no source other than the Bible records the atrocity. The town was that small. Spiritually, the family of Jesus and the city of His birth were rich. But not in the eyes of those who crave power.

To understand the Incarnation we need to put it into perspective. Imagine living in a town where the biggest claim to fame is that you live only 50 miles from the nearest Wal-Mart. Also, your family consists of good people but you aren't wealthy. You live in a trailer for two, but you are a family of ten. By the way, did I mention you were the family dog? Now when I say "dog," I don't mean Pit Bull or Doberman. You're a Chihuahua and, no, you can't say, "Yo Quiero Taco Bell!" Please understand I am not trying to be insulting or insensitive to the Person of Jesus whom we love and worship. I am simply seeking to underscore the humility it took for God the Son to become human. That's why Paul admonishes every believer to have the mind of Christ in Philippians 2…

> **Your attitude should be the same as that of**
> **Christ Jesus: Who, being in very nature God, did**

not consider equality with God something to be grasped, but made himself nothing, taking the very nature of a servant, being made in human likeness. And being found in appearance as a man, he humbled himself and became obedient to death—even death on a cross!

Jesus understood the role that was His to play in the story that God is telling. Humility allows me to fulfill my role with excellence and not feel the need to want someone else's position or place. It allows me to live with gratitude for what God has already done. Humility is knowing who I am in light of who God is, yet I wonder how many of us don't know ourselves because we are trying to live out someone else's role. I think of David when he tried out Saul's armor. I'm sure it was a thrill to put on the King's battle gear. I'm sure it would be like wearing an authentic Michael Jordan number 23 jersey and hitting the court for a pick up basketball game. Yet David didn't see value in wearing someone else's number. Instead, he chose to humbly use the gifts that God had given him to do the will of God. He faced Goliath with just his slingshot and a few stones. That's the heart of those who are consumed by God. They want to be like Jesus in every way, so when something is done that is good, pure, or noble, the glory will not belong to us, the "snowplows." Instead, the glory will belong to the One whom we prepare the way for. The reality is, in the end, if no one remembers our names, it isn't going to matter. But there is one Name that needs to be remembered. That's where Paul finishes his thoughts on humility…

Therefore God exalted him to the highest place and gave him the name that is above every name, that at the name of Jesus every knee should bow, in heaven and on earth and under the earth, and every tongue confess that Jesus Christ is Lord, to the glory of God the Father.

(PHILIPPIANS 2:9-11 NIV)

BOTTOM OF THE ORDER

When I was playing baseball I went into a severe slump that caused me to move from the clean up (fourth hitter) spot all the way down to the bottom of the hitting order. Before the game started, my coach pulled me aside and said, "Bob, don't worry about where you bat in the lineup. I'm doing what's best for the team. Simply do your best and everything will work out." Then my moment came. It was my turn at the plate. We were behind by a run and there was a man on second. I was so nervous because I wasn't hitting well and the team needed me. The pitch came and I clobbered it! I rounded first and it got past the center fielder. So I hustled and turned my base hit into a double. The next batter got a hit and the center fielder let the ball get past him again (big problems in center field) and I ran for home. There was a play at that plate and I was…safe! My team took the lead and we eventually won the game. I remember the blue pants I wore got grass stains that never came out and I didn't care because I did it for my team. I watched many other kids stomp their feet, cry like babies, and even quit their teams because they didn't get to play the game on their terms. I am so glad my dad taught me to always think of the team before myself.

That's what our heavenly Father wants us to learn. He wants us to think of the kingdom before we think of ourselves. John the Baptist rightly reflected the humility of Jesus and it made him someone that God could use. How? He knew his role. Do you want to be used by God like John the Baptist was? Do you want to be a catalyst for change and live a revolutionary life? I think we all do. It will take an honest assessment of our gifts, and leaving pride at the door. For a husband, it means recognizing the promotion you've been seeking isn't the answer to your problems; understanding your role in God's purpose for this world is. To a wife, that might mean realizing God's structure for the home and allowing your husband to lead. It will be a freeing experience for you because you have accepted your role in God's story. It means teenagers who find a way to trust their parents' decisions and respect their role; they find peace and safety. It's Christians like John the Baptist that learn their roles in God's story and decide to humble themselves in the sight of God and as the Bible says, "...*He will be the one to lift you up" (James 4:10)* to greater victories and greater heights. John is proof that greatness is never found in thinking of ourselves first. It is found by seeing yourself in light of who God is and celebrating that by being the person God has created you to be.

CHAPTER 05

floor model

chapter 05//**floor model**

My wife knows that she is the most important person in the world to me, but there is now serious competition. My niece Sarah is running at a close second.

SHE ABSOLUTELY
    MEANS THE WORLD
TO CAREY AND I.

The reason is because not only is she the cutest six year old ever, I think she's the funniest six year old I have ever known. I mean she really has a great sense of humor. The kind of humor where you know it takes major brainpower to craft a story and deliver the punch line. I surprised her at school a couple of months ago with a McDonald's Happy Meal for lunch. She was so surprised to see me! We spent her entire lunch hour laughing. But the amazing part was that we were laughing at her jokes. Like when she started telling me a story about what her mom had been teaching her from the Bible. She learned the story about Jesus healing a leper. So her mom asked her, "Sarah, do you know what a leper is?" She said, "Yeah. It's kind of like a cheetah." She told me that and we both died laughing. I've lost about 70 pounds over the last several months and when I had first started shedding some weight, people in our church were so kind and encouraging to me. But Sarah found it time to joke. I was carrying her after a church service and she grabbed my cheeks and said, "Uncle Bobby, you're chubby!" (Did I mention she's also truthful to a fault?)

But I've noticed something as of late. I have this suspicion that she likes Carey more than me and, frankly, it kind of bothers me. In fact, when I saw Sarah recently at a birthday party I said "hi" to her and the first words she said to me were, "Where's Carey?" I'm thinking, "Girl, that's just rude! I'm here now. Talk to Carey later!" But I told her where she was and Sarah just walked right past me to find Carey. Sarah's mom told me that sometimes she cries because she misses Carey. So I gently asked, "Did she cry for me?" Her mom said, "Not so much." Whenever she stays at our house, if there's a problem she wants to find Carey. I have tried to show her that I am a grown up and am capable of solving some of life's basic problems as well, but she's not convinced. Even if I prove my case that I am able to handle the situation, she still wants Carey and will accept no substitute. I plead with her and try to prove my competence in this world by saying, "Yes Sarah, I can fill up the cup with water so you can use the water colors!" She says she wants Carey to do it.

Why is it that when someone elects to tell us something we don't want to hear, it is like they are blowing a silent whistle that only dogs can hear because we cannot hear or receive what they are saying? Yet when someone that we trust says tough words, even if the message is difficult to accept, we seem to acknowledge their counsel and the need to change. There is something about a person's acceptance and love that draws us to them. Think about those people in your life that, like Carey is to Sarah, you call on when you have a problem. These are the people we want to talk to, be with, have pray for us, and comfort us. If there is correction that needs to happen in our lives, we would rather hear it from them than anyone else. I see this with husbands and wives all the time. A wife will share a thought or an idea with her husband and for some reason, he will not believe it. It doesn't matter if she is quoting the Bible itself, he believes there is another way. He goes to work and a coworker says the same thing and it is like fresh revelation from heaven! How does the story end? He goes home and tells his wife about the great idea that his buddy at work had, and she reminds him that she's been pleading with him and saying the same thing for the last two months! So what does this smart husband do?

(HERE'S A LITTLE HINT, GUYS.)

He says, "Well, Honey, he was just reinforcing and confirming the truth that you shared with me! Doesn't the Bible say that everything should be confirmed by at least two or three witnesses?"

People hear insight, correction, or ideas from those they believe are looking out for their best interests, and who have pure motives in sharing. That's why I say "No" to all telemarketing callers no matter what they are selling. They could tell me they are sending me a box of $100 bills and they just want to confirm my mailing address; my answer is still "No!" Why? Because of one word: motive. Motive is the reason you believe the people you trust and it is why people flocked to John the Baptist. Plain and simple, people left institutional religion and went out to the desert to see John because he was an example of the life that he offered. This principle in John's life works in every area of our lives where we want people to listen. Too many times, we as Christians are offering something that we ourselves don't possess and then we wonder why those that don't follow Jesus won't respond. It's like when Mark, our Youth Pastor, ordered satellite TV. He had a problem so he called Customer Service and asked the woman on the other end of the phone how having satellite TV has worked for her. Much to Mark's dismay, the agent said she had no idea because she didn't have satellite TV, she had cable! That doesn't breed much confidence! In fact, it's downright scary. Yet this is what many Christians do. We tell people how to live but we don't live that way ourselves. Then we wonder why people aren't drawn to us. It's because our life should be "Exhibit A" of what God can do. Then, when our lives and our message match up, people will seek us out because they recognize that the life we offer is the life we are living.

WE TELL PEOPLE HOW TO LIVE BUT WE DON'T LIVE THAT WAY OURSELVES.

Do you remember the TV show, "Let's Make a Deal?" I have only seen reruns, but the host, Monty Hall, would have someone choose door number one, two, or three. Of course, no one knew what was behind each door. So they could either choose a door or accept a deal. The people in John's day had a couple of doors to choose from, but unlike TV game shows they got to look behind the curtain and see if it was worth accepting of not. The problem was people were choosing door number three and it was making doors number one and two mad! So doors number one and two decided to show up and see what door number three was doing to get everyone to choose him.

In those days John the Baptist began preaching in the Judean wilderness. His message was, "Turn from your sins and turn to God, because the Kingdom of Heaven is near." Isaiah had spoken of John when he said, "He is a voice shouting in the wilderness: `Prepare a pathway for the Lord's coming! Make a straight road for him!'" John's clothes were woven from camel hair, and he wore a leather belt; his food was locusts and wild honey. People from Jerusalem and from every section of Judea and from all over the Jordan Valley went out to the wilderness to hear him preach. And when they confessed their sins, he baptized them in the Jordan River. But when he saw many Pharisees and Sadducees coming to be baptized, he denounced them. "You brood of snakes!" he exclaimed. "Who warned you to flee God's coming judgment? Prove by the way you live that you have really turned from your sins and turned to God. Don't just say, 'We're safe-- we're the descendants of Abraham.' That proves nothing. God can change these stones here into children of Abraham. Even now the ax of God's judgment is poised, ready to sever your roots. Yes, every tree that does not produce good fruit

will be chopped down and thrown into the fire."
(MATTHEW 3:1-10 NLT)

EVEN MANNEQUINS LIE!

I was in the Gap recently looking for a shirt. I saw one I liked, grabbed a potentially fitting size and hit the dressing room. But as I tried it on, I said to Carey, "Why is it that the shirts here never fit me like they fit the mannequins?" She looked as though I was referring to size and gave me the eyes that said, "When you're shaped like a snowman, clothes don't fit that well." So I said, "Not the size, the fit of the shirt! How come the mannequins never have bunches of material popping out on the sides?" So I left the fitting room wearing the shirt and there, the Gap's lies were exposed! I went out only to find pins on the shirts on the mannequins holding the material back! I looked around to see who would pay for the lies they have been telling the public and feel my wrath! So I put the shirt back and left because they had no real example of what they were offering. They were pinning back what they were offering to hide what they really had. So I went to Express (For Men), and there I found something completely different. I discovered a place where the shirts fit exactly the way they look on the mannequins. So I bought my shirt there because their examples revealed what they really offered.

There were two groups on the shore of the Jordan River watching John, and the burning question they were wondering was why no one was interested in them. These two groups did not get along famously, but they both walked many miles to find out what John was doing because people were going to him and not them. These were the religious people. They had the cool religious clothes, the authority, and even fancy buildings to meet in. But even with all of that, they still had nothing that people wanted because they weren't examples of the life they offered. Here is what I mean…

SPLIT PERSONALITY DISORDER

The first group was the Sadducees. The Sadducees were the power brokers in ancient Israel even though they were by far the smallest of all the Jewish sects. This group oversaw the Temple, the sacrifices, and the worship therein, mostly because they claimed to have been descended from Zadok, the high priest during the time of Solomon. In Jesus' time, the high priest was a Sadducee, as was most of the 70-member Jewish Supreme Court called the Sanhedrin. During the time in history when the Roman Empire was wielding their power throughout the known world, they found groups within each culture to support who would keep the "Pax Romana" or peace in that region. This is where the Sadducees agreed to be Roman stooges. They became corrupt in their dealing and the common people saw them as such. Religiously, the Sadducees were very conservative; they believed only in the Torah. They saw no need for the Psalms, the Prophets, or the books of history. They believed what God said to Moses as recorded in the Torah was all that God had truly spoken. Thus they rejected the oral traditions, which the Pharisees accepted. They also did not believe in an afterlife or a resurrection. While being extremely conservative religiously, Sadducees were culturally liberal. They loved the Greco-Roman culture, and many of the Sadducees went as far as to adopt Greek names. It is said that Sadducees were notorious for entering the Gymnasium (The English word comes from the Greek word Gumnos, which means "naked"[9]), which was a place devoted to athletic competition in the nude. In fact, the Apocryphal book of 1 Maccabees tells us that a gymnasium was built in Jerusalem.

> In those days there appeared in Israel men who were breakers of the law, and they seduced many people, saying: "Let us go and make an alliance with the Gentiles all around us; since we separated from them, many evils have come upon us." The proposal was agreeable; some from among the people promptly went to the king, and he authorized them to introduce the way of living of the Gentiles. Thereupon they built a gymnasium in Jerusalem according to the Gentile custom. They covered over the mark of their circumcision and abandoned the holy covenant; they allied themselves with the Gentiles and sold themselves to wrongdoing.

(1 MACCABEES 1:11-15)[10]

Even more disturbing is that the book of 2 Maccabees tells us that so many young priests were going to the gymnasium that the services in the Temple were being neglected.[11] So while the Sadducees were Jewish religiously, their faith had no bearing as to how they lived their lives. Yet they still didn't understand why more people didn't want to be like them. They did not realize that people want to see is something real, and that they should have been an example of the life they offered, but they were not even close. They were to the religious community what Sydney Bristow is to the hit TV show, "Alias." They were double agents—people who made their living existing in two worlds. The only difference is on "Alias," being a double agent makes Sydney a hero. In the real world, living a double life makes you a hypocrite. Their existence was one where you paid God lip service at the Temple, but you lived every other day of your life as you pleased. This is the kind of person who is the reason many people don't believe in Jesus and walk with Him. We share about life in Christ with others, and we could write the script because we have heard it so many times. They say, "But I knew a Christian once who said they were a believer, but they _____ ___!" Every time, the fill in the blank part is different, but the story is the same. It's the tale of the "says one thing, but does another" Christian. These people frustrate me to no end because not only are they themselves not walking with God; they are an obstruction for others to walk with Him. I plead with these people to not even call themselves Christians.

I TOLD MY CHURCH RECENTLY,
    "IF YOU AREN'T GOING TO
WALK WITH GOD,
        DON'T CALL
YOURSELF A CHRISTIAN.
TELL PEOPLE YOU'RE PART OF
THE CIRCUS OR SOMETHING,
BUT JUST LEAVE JESUS OUT OF
IT BECAUSE
IT'S SADDUCEE-LIKE PEOPLE
THAT GIVE CHRISTIANS A BAD
NAME!"

What's interesting is that this same hypocrisy enraged many of the orthodox Jews living in this time and a group split from them. This group gave themselves the names, "The Separated Ones"[12] or Pharisees...

CONDO COMMANDO

If you have ever lived in an apartment building, condominium, or townhouse, then you will understand the story I am about to tell you because every one of these housing developments has at least one Condo Commando! What is a Condo Commando, you might ask? This is a person or group of people that have nothing better to do than to find out who is violating what ordinance in the list of rules for living in their so called "paradise." This is the group that calls you when you take your trash out 15 minutes before the allotted time. This Illuminati-like organization leaves nasty notes on your door if your trashcan is out too long or your weeds aren't pulled, or if there are too many cars parked outside of your house. Several months ago, we had a few people over to our home and there were several cars parked outside. Now, I live at the end of a row of houses, which means I am at a dead end. No cars drive in front of my house unless, of course, you are coming to my house! So these cars were not blocking anyone, but this didn't stop a Condo Commando Pharisee from putting notes on the cars in front of the house. The best part is that since the weather was overcast and there was a chance of rain, the person decided to cover each note that they put on each car with Saran wrap. This way, the nasty letter wouldn't be damaged by any unforeseen precipitation! This is exactly who the Pharisees were. They

THE BEST PART IS THAT SINCE THE WEATHER WAS OVERCAST AND THERE WAS A CHANCE OF RAIN, THE PERSON DECIDED TO COVER EACH NOTE THAT THEY PUT ON EACH CAR WITH SARAN WRAP. THIS WAY, THE NASTY LETTER WOULDN'T BE DAMAGED BY ANY UNFORESEEN PRECIPITATION! THIS IS EXACTLY WHO THE PHARISEES WERE.

were the rule makers and the scorekeepers. They heavily influenced synagogue worship and were deeply respected by many of the people because of their piety, which Jesus denounced as "hypocrisy." Religiously, the Pharisees were the equivalent to modern-day Evangelicals. They believed in the entire Old Testament, but they also held to the oral traditions, which according to tradition was given to Moses by God on Mount Sinai. The oral tradition also comprised the teachings of the scribes and sages throughout the history of Judaism. This means, not only did the Pharisees have to follow the 613 Old Testament laws, they also had thousands of other laws that were part of the oral tradition or were interpretations of what the sages believed the verses meant. Due to the complexity of this system, the standard they set was impossible to meet, and anyone who didn't meet their expectations was quite simply a loser! Jesus had many confrontations with the Pharisees but usually it was not over their interpretation of Scripture, instead it was in their implementation of Scripture. Here's an example of one such confrontation:

> The Pharisees and some of the teachers of the law who had come from Jerusalem gathered around Jesus and saw some of his disciples eating food with hands that were "unclean," that is, unwashed. (The Pharisees and all the Jews do not eat unless they give their hands a ceremonial washing, holding to the tradition of the elders. When they come from the marketplace they do not eat unless they wash. And they observe many other traditions, such as the washing of cups, pitchers and kettles.) So the Pharisees and teachers of the law asked Jesus, "Why don't your disciples live according to the tradition of the elders instead of eating their food with 'unclean' hands?" He replied, "Isaiah was right when he prophesied about you hypocrites; as it is written: 'These people honor me with their lips, but their hearts are far from me. They worship me in vain; their teachings are but rules taught by men.' You have let go of the commands of God and

are holding on to the traditions of men." And he said to them: "You have a fine way of setting aside the commands of God in order to observe your own traditions! For Moses said, 'Honor your father and your mother,' and, 'Anyone who curses his father or mother must be put to death.' But you say that if a man says to his father or mother: 'Whatever help you might otherwise have received from me is Corban' (that is, a gift devoted to God), then you no longer let him do anything for his father or mother. Thus you nullify the word of God by your tradition that you have handed down. And you do many things like that."

(MARK 7:1-13 NIV)

Jesus' problem with the Pharisees was that they created rules that nullified God's original meaning. Consider the passage you just read. The Pharisees were giving Jesus a hard time because His disciples did not wash their hands in the ceremonial way. So Jesus challenged the Pharisees in how they loved to devise traditions that got so involved that the original meaning God intended was lost. So what is "Corban?" "Corban" is a word the Pharisees created which means, "Gift to God."[13] What this did was create an escape clause to allow a person to not obey the Bible and honor their parents. So if you saw your parents in need, or if your parents asked you for help, you could simply say, "I wish I could help you, but I declared all of my possessions as Corban." What was this declaration? It was simply telling God that everything you owned belonged to Him. Doesn't that sound spiritual? The interesting part is that a person didn't have to give anything away, help the poor, or alter his or her lifestyle one iota. It simply meant that all of your possessions were "technically" no longer yours, but you still did with them as you pleased. So this system developed as a way for the Pharisees to escape helping their parents in their time of need. It doesn't sound very spiritual anymore, does it?

Have you ever met a person like this? A Condo Commando for Jesus, who creates rules for everyone to follow that have nothing to do with the Bible, yet preaches his or her convictions and opinions as inspired text. This is the type of person who says categorical statements like, "The Bible says women should not wear makeup!" I have personally been asked this question a number of times, and I say what I heard the famed preacher Dr. J. Vernon McGee say: "If the barn needs painting, paint it!" The Condo Commando Pharisee demands an answer to the question, "Should a Christian wear a one piece or two piece swimsuit?" I have personally chosen to wear a one piece, but that's just me. They say, "Christians shouldn't dance." So people have asked me that question as well, wanting to know what's right. I always say, "From what I've seen when it comes to Christians and dancing, some can and some can't."

SUPERMODELS WANTED

People were choosing door number three because John the Baptist had something in his life that others wanted duplicated in their lives. John was offering something they had forgotten. He was offering freely an opportunity to know and experience God that was not about rituals and religion. Instead, he offered a personal relationship with Jesus Christ. With so many people coming to hear John, I am sure there were naysayers thinking John had a watered down message. You can judge for yourself, but I don't think so because his message seemed pretty straightforward...

> **In those days John the Baptist came, preaching in the Desert of Judea and saying, "Repent, for the kingdom of heaven is near."**
> (MATTHEW 3:1-2 NIV)

John's call to commitment was radical and life altering. The other two groups had managed to take God out the equation of their lives so they could do what they pleased. John called people out of the shadows and into the light. He called individuals from the shores of indecision to the waters of commitment through baptism. People are not afraid of commitment. People are simply afraid of giving their lives to a cause that won't mean anything after they are gone. John was challenging people to live the adventure and commit themselves to God, who would be able to ignite a fire in them that could touch the world. I believe the church that I have the privilege of pastoring is the best illustration of this point. There are so many other churches in our area that have better facilities, expensive organs, colorful robes and pew Bibles so you don't even have to bring your own when you come. But for some reason, they drive past those plush facilities to come to a movie theatre where more than once my feet have stuck to the floor due to the oil from the popcorn that wasn't mopped up properly. This shows me something about the people that come to Calvary Fellowship.

IT SHOWS ME THAT PEOPLE AREN'T INTERESTED IN EXTERNALS AS MUCH AS THEY ARE INTERESTED IN BEING A PART OF A COMMUNITY OF BELIEVERS THAT ARE FOLLOWING JESUS WITH A SINCERE DESIRE TO WALK WITH GOD.

That is what people are looking for—others who are the example of the life they offer, and that is why John started a revolution in his world.

I had heard the Gospel many times before the day I prayed to receive Jesus as my Savior, but I had never responded until someone I trusted that had a real relationship with God shared the Gospel with me. I went to visit my brother in Boston with a girl named Carey that I was dating at the time. We stayed at my brother's house for two weeks and I watched the change that had taken place in his life. I remembered him before entering into a relationship with God and the kind of life he lived. But in those two weeks, I witnessed firsthand a faith that was real and authentic. So two days before we left to come home to Florida, I asked my brother Billy some questions about the Christian life and the conversation ended when Carey and I prayed to receive Jesus as our Savior. I knew about God but I didn't know God the way he did and I wanted to. In fact, I needed to. My brother had become a John the Baptist floor model for me and my life has never been the same.

Just like me, there are countless lives that are looking to be changed by the power of one life that is completely sold out to the cause of Jesus Christ. If you don't believe that one person can make a difference, ask the U.S. Army which has invested millions of dollars into its advertising campaign, "An Army of One." God is looking for people who are willing to be supermodels. Not in the fashion world, where you get millions of dollars to wear the latest clothing lines at the most beautiful places on the planet. Instead, God is looking for people who will be supermodels of what it means to follow Jesus in the real world where there are countless people who have given up on religion, but not on God; where many have lost faith in the institutional approach to God, but are ever-ready to learn of a real relationship with a loving heavenly Father. God is looking for people who are willing to live the kind of life where they can say, like the Apostle Paul, *"And you should follow my example, just as I follow Christ's" (1 Corinthians 11:1 NLT).* Are there any takers to "strike a pose?"

CHAPTER 06

chapter 06//watermark

People have weird tastes, especially when it comes to food. Some friends of mine took me to a restaurant in Coral Gables and it was awesome. But my first time looking through the menu was like reading a French dictionary. It was the kind of high-end restaurant that only Miami can give you. It was fusion style cuisine that blends Caribbean, Latin, and American flavors all on your plate. I wasn't too excited about it but, once I ordered, it was amazing. I knew I had chosen wisely because of all the dishes I sampled, the only dish I really loved was the one I ordered. I don't know if you've ever felt that way in a restaurant—like you somehow dodged a bullet. While everything else I tried was good, it wasn't what I'd want to spend my evening eating. That's what makes people individuals. We all have different tastes and likings. That's why there are some foods or combinations of foods that you love and you are the only person on planet earth who loves them. But there are other foods that if you had the choice, you'd pick rat poison over a plate of _____. For example, my wife loves the taste of Coke and milk mixed. I've tried counseling, therapy, interventions, but she still loves it. I think it's just plain nasty! If Carey has a Coke by itself, she'll put ice in it and wait for the ice to melt to water it down. For most people, that happens by accident, but she sets out to do it. I'm not immune to the weird factor either. I know it sounds disgusting, but I really like the taste of cough medicine. It seems disgusting, but when I get sick, cherry flavored Robitussin is all I need. Most people gag when they have to take cough medicine. I, on the other hand, have been known to chug it from the bottle from time to time.

But I'm always interested in other's tastes for varieties of life. Like I don't understand how people can pay money to watch a movie that's tragic. Most of us just need to get out of bed in the morning to experience that for free. If you want me to never see a movie, just say these words, "It's really sad." Case closed. This bird has flown. I'm done. If it doesn't have explosions, funny dialogue, or an epic adventure, count me out.

FOUR WEDDINGS AND A FUNERAL

In light of that, I do have one weird thing about me that not many people understand. I like funerals. I know that sounds morbid because most people don't. In fact, they try to go a lifetime without attending one, but I like them. Now let me clarify before you label me as some kind of mental case. I like officiating funerals. I don't like it when people I love pass away and I'm not looking forward to being the name on the program at my own memorial service. Yet, as a pastor, two of my "extracurricular" activities are weddings and funerals. All pastors have a preference as to which they prefer. The problem is, I've never met anyone who likes funerals more than weddings…except for me. So the question you want to know is, "Why?" I'll explain by asking you a question: What do you remember the pastor saying at the last wedding you attended outside of the usual "I do" stuff? Don't remember? That is precisely my point. The pastor could have been reading the phone book and most of us would have never known the difference because no one cares what the pastor says at weddings.

BUT AT A FUNERAL, WE ARE HANGING ON EVERY WORD BECAUSE WE ARE LOOKING FOR GOD IN THOSE TIMES. SOMETIMES A SIMPLE BIBLE VERSE CAN BE THE DIFFERENCE BETWEEN HOPE AND DESPAIR. SO I GUESS I LIKE THE ROLE THAT I PLAY IN FUNERALS BETTER BECAUSE I FEEL LIKE I'M MAKING A DIFFERENCE.

Now don't get me wrong, I don't like the sad part of funerals. In fact, I hate that part. I hate seeing people cry and saying goodbye to someone they love. It kills me inside. But I love the fact that people are really open to God in those moments. It shows us that we aren't immortal and we are going to see our Maker someday. In contrast, I don't hate weddings. I love the joy, the commitments that are made, etc… I appreciate the families (even the crazy ones) who want everything just perfect for this most special of days. In fact, I know there's a God because there's a phenomenon to me that is unexplainable. I have never seen an ugly bride. Every bride I have ever seen has been stunningly beautiful. I have seen plenty of ugly wives in my life, but never an ugly bride. That's why I wish I could fuse the joy of weddings with the sobriety of funerals. Maybe at our next funeral, we could all get an expensive ring as we ponder life and mortality. Or at our next wedding, we could mourn the death of two individual people and celebrate the birth of a new couple committing their lives to each other. But I guess that might be like mixing Coke and milk; separate they're good, but together it wouldn't have a huge mass appeal. Then I started thinking that there is a place where the two meet. An event that symbolizes death but celebrates commitment…it's called baptism.

THE WATER BOY

If you're like me, you might have a mixed up view of what baptism is because of your background or the church you grew up in. In my particular childhood tradition, baptism was something infants did to become part of a religion and ensure they would go to heaven.

MAYBE AT OUR NEXT FUNERAL, WE COULD ALL GET AN EXPENSIVE RING AS WE PONDER LIFE AND MORTALITY. OR AT OUR NEXT WEDDING, WE COULD MOURN THE DEATH OF TWO INDIVIDUAL PEOPLE AND CELEBRATE THE BIRTH OF A NEW COUPLE COMMITTING THEIR LIVES TO EACH OTHER.

Yet when I became a Christian, I soon discovered that isn't exactly what the Bible teaches. What I want us to experience together is one of the most important events in history. It's a baptism service that took place at the Jordan River 2,000 years ago. This baptism had nothing to do with religion or a ritual that marked my place in heaven because I got soaked inside of a church building. Instead, it shows us what baptism really is: that baptism is the mark of a life committed to God. That's why any Christian would want to get baptized. Jesus commanded us as His disciples to be baptized so it would serve as an outward symbol of an inward commitment. It would put the world on notice that we were leaving our old lives behind and embracing the lives that God has for us. And it would serve as a memorial to us of the day we fully committed ourselves to God. That's why Jesus was standing on the banks of the Jordan River that day. He was there to show us what baptism was all about. So where does Jesus go to get baptized? Perhaps better put, to whom does Jesus go? He went to John the Baptist. To a man that was consumed by God and was leading others to be the same. It is here that we find our model of what baptism is and why it should be an element in the life of every person that desires to be a disciple of Jesus.

> Then Jesus came from Galilee to the Jordan to
> be baptized by John. But John tried to deter
> him, saying, "I need to be baptized by you, and
> do you come to me?" Jesus replied, "Let it be
> so now; it is proper for us to do this to fulfill all
> righteousness." Then John consented. As soon as
> Jesus was baptized, he went up out of the water.
> At that moment heaven was opened, and he saw
> the Spirit of God descending like a dove and
> lighting on him. And a voice from heaven said,
> "This is my Son, whom I love; with him I am well
> pleased."
> (MATTHEW 3:13-17 NIV)

My niece, Sarah, is like a daughter to me. It's amazing how much you can love someone even though they probably don't totally understand it. But I love spending time with her because she has developed an amazing sense of humor and she is really artistic. I was talking to her recently about her future and how when she goes to college she can live with Carey and I, and she can come and work at the church (a shameless display of nepotism at its best).

SHE HASN'T DECIDED IF THAT'S THE RIGHT CHOICE FOR HER.
LUCKILY, I STILL HAVE 12 YEARS TO TALK HER INTO IT.

So Sarah and I were having one of our conversations a few months ago and I asked her when she had lunch at school because I wanted to visit her someday. So she said, "Noon." A couple of weeks later, I was in the neighborhood and I decided to drop by and see her during her lunchtime. The only problem was, she was nowhere to be found. I talked to a teacher in the lunchroom and asked where the Kindergarten class was. She said, "Sorry, that class has lunch from 11:00 to 11:30." Then it hit me: She's five years old and that means she doesn't know how to tell time!

I think that's how John must have felt when Jesus showed up to be baptized. It was like asking him, "What time do you have lunch?" John is stunned and replies, "I can't tell time. You should be the one telling me when I have lunch!" But Jesus was modeling something for us. He was showing us what the heart of baptism is all about. It's the mark of a life committed to God. In the Jewish culture, people would wash in what was called a "Mikveh." This was a ritual bath where you would immerse yourself to be cleansed ceremonially so you could go and worship at the temple in Jerusalem. This was especially used as part of a ritual for those that were not Jewish and were converting to Judaism. They would be baptized as a sign of dying to their old lives and entering into a new relationship with Yahweh, the God of Israel. But there was a little problem—John was baptizing Jewish people. He was telling them to repent because the kingdom of God was at hand, and that their Jewish heritage wasn't proof that they walked with God. So these committed people were baptized to signify their desire to really walk with God. That's why the religious people were angry. Baptizing Jews was outrageous—it was also unheard of! He was the only person doing this. That's how John got his nickname: "Yohanan the Baptizo" or John the Baptist. Lest you think there's a denominational thing going on here, literally he was called John the Immerser.[14] The Greek has a word for immerse and another word for sprinkle. "Baptizo" means to immerse.[15] If Matthew wanted to let us know that John sprinkled people, he would have used another word: "Rhantizo."[16] I joke around with pastors who believe in sprinkling and I tell them that John was called the immerser, not "Rain Man."

Yet, Jesus wanting to be immersed was a problem for John. Remember John is telling people to repent, but Jesus had nothing to repent of. He's God. He doesn't have sins to confess or shameful deeds to wash away. This is why John was stuck like a deer caught in the headlights. I understand this feeling. I remember being asked to teach at a Leadership Conference and my pastor introduced me and then sat down and started taking notes! I asked myself, "What's wrong with this picture?" I felt like a high school basketball coach teaching teenagers the fundamentals of the game and Shaquille O'Neal shows up and wants to be part of the class. You'd say, "I think you should teach me!" (Unless it was the day we were learning to shoot free throws.) But Jesus said, "I want to be baptized because it fulfills what God requires." Only then does John agree to baptize Him. The issue for Jesus was to obey His Father and do what was right. There is something that happens when a person makes a decision to be baptized. They aren't just deciding to get wet; they are dying to the old way of life and craving to live the abundant life that Jesus offers.

> **Or have you forgotten that when we became Christians and were baptized to become one with Christ Jesus, we died with him? For we died and were buried with Christ by baptism. And just as Christ was raised from the dead by the glorious power of the Father, now we also may live new lives.**
> (ROMANS 6:3-4 NLT)

MAY I SEE SOME IDENTIFICATION?

Being baptized is about deciding to be numbered with the disciples of Jesus, not getting wet or performing some ritual. You see, people won't have a problem with someone coming to church occasionally. But you tell your friends that aren't Christians that you are getting baptized and they are going to think that you're taking this "Jesus" thing too far. Do you know why? Because they recognize how important baptism is even though many in the church don't.

> **Therefore, go and make disciples of all the nations, baptizing them in the name of the Father and the Son and the Holy Spirit. Teach these new disciples to obey all the commands I have given you. And be sure of this: I am with you always, even to the end of the age.**
> (MATTHEW 28:19-20 NLT)

Jesus links baptism with following Him. The issue isn't, "Can I still go to heaven if I'm not baptized?" The thief on the cross did, but he never had the chance to be baptized. If they took him down from the cross and said, "Yes, that robbery was just a misunderstanding. Please accept our deepest apologies and have a nice day." I'm going to go out on a limb and say he would have gotten baptized. The issue is if you are a disciple of Jesus, you will gladly obey Him in this simple, yet powerful act. I watch Christians go years without being baptized because they don't think it's a big deal. I say, "Jesus asks us to do this. That makes it a big deal!" Many times these are the same people who are praying about God's will because they don't know what to do. We're never going to figure out what God wants us to do if we haven't done what we know for sure He's already asked us to do. Some say, "Well, I was baptized as an infant?" So was I. But that's not what Jesus is talking about.

> **...Baptism is not a removal of dirt from your body; it is an appeal to God from a clean conscience.**
> (1 PETER 3:21 NLT)

I have pictures of my infant baptism and I wasn't appealing anything to God except for my lungs, because it looks like I was screaming the whole time. I don't remember it and it didn't signify anything in my life. So I personally cannot say I have obeyed Jesus in this area when that baptism was not of my own volition. I think sometimes we hesitate because we're scared. Because there's something inside of us that knows something happens when we go into the waters of baptism. I can tell you from personal experience, people don't leave the same if they really mean it. People repent before God, declare their faith in Jesus, and commit to living out His purposes for their lives. I have had people hand me packs of cigarettes in the water just prior to them being baptized. They quit right on the spot – no patch, no gum, no hypnosis, nothing. It was just a commitment to live for God starting from that moment. Once, during a baptism service, I had a man who wanted to be baptized hand me his cigarettes while we were in the water. This baptism was at the ocean, so I put them in my pocket because I felt that being a litterbug during a baptism wasn't the most spiritual thing to do. My intention was to keep them in my pocket until I got out of the water and then throw them out. Unfortunately, I forgot they were in my pocket. So I got home and later that afternoon Carey was washing the clothes I wore at the baptism and she found a soaked pack of Marlboro's in my pocket. She said, "Bob, is there something about you that I don't know about?" So I told her the story, we shared a smoke and went our merry way (just kidding). She threw them out. That's all…

But I believe something happens when someone who has prayed to receive Jesus decides to get watermarked by baptism. It shows their desire to live a revolutionary life by adding that element to their lives that Jesus and John had. I was baptized when I had been a Christian for about four months, but in 1999 I was in Israel at the very spot where John baptized Jesus and I had baptized 25 or 30 people who were part of our tour group. At the end of the baptism service, I asked the other pastors to baptize me because I believed God was calling me to do something great. He was calling me to come to Miami to start a church. I was enjoying a good life. I worked at a big church and ran a college full of students whose sole desire was to serve God. It was great. Yet I felt God stirring me and I couldn't shake it. So at that moment in the Jordan River, I did what Jesus did in that same spot. I decided to get consumed by God. I decided to live a life that wasn't comfortable, but instead was revolutionary. It's what God calls every person who calls Jesus "Lord" to do. He calls them to get watermarked and start a revolution in their world by starting one in their own lives first. It's at that moment that you will hear the words that Jesus heard. The words of your loving, heavenly Father who will look from heaven and say, "That's my son in whom I am well pleased."

CHAPTER 07

vending machine

chapter 07//**vending machine**

I don't know what you think of when you hear the words, "Vending Machine?" Most of us think of Snickers, Three Musketeers, Life Savers, Zingers (imitation Twinkies), and those square orange crackers with peanut butter in the middle. Yet what I have learned is that the vending machine industry is branching out. So much so, that you can go to England, stop at a vending machine and pick up an umbrella! Or next time you are in Japan, stop by the beer vending machine (they are on the street, by the way) and grab a cold one. What is bizarre to me is that in Japan there are also egg vending machines. Yes, you read that correctly – eggs. So I have this idea as to what happens in Japan even though I've never been there: people buy beer on the street from the beer vending machines. Then, once they are totally plastered, they start shouting obscenities at each other and in their fury they go and buy a dozen eggs at the egg vending machine and "egg" each other! I have this image of Japanese streets being filled with beer cans and eggshells. I know it's not true, but it's fun to think about.

Believe it or not, America has its own set of unique vending machines. I have a picture of a Reebok vending machine where if you realize that you aren't wearing any shoes, you can put up a new pair of "kicks" before you go running. If you are ever bored at the Atlanta airport, don't worry because the iPod vending machine is there. Just put in $300 in quarters and you'll be listening to your favorite song in no time!

GOD THE VENDOR?

We have figured out how to put most of life into a vending machine because that's how we like it. Think about it: it is a totally fair system.

A PERSON WALKS UP,
PUTS IN MONEY,
MAKES A SELECTION,
AND THE MACHINE
     DELIVERS A TREAT.
WE WANT ALL OF LIFE
   TO BE LIKE THIS,
BUT MOST IMPORTANTLY,
WE WANT OUR RELATIONSHIP
     WITH GOD
       TO BE LIKE THIS AS WELL.

We want to be able to put in a certain amount of money, effort, energy, or time and the result will be that God does everything we ask of Him. Now, of course we would never say this publicly, but internally we want it to be the case. Why do I think this? It is because all of us have been cheated by a vending machine in the past. I bet you remember the day. You had your last seventy-five cents in your pocket and you were hungry, looking for a sugary treat to calm your grumbling and complaining stomach. So you walked up to the vending machine and noticed a welcomed friend. You put your coins in and you watched with dire anticipation as that antiquated metal coil started turning to release the answer to all of your hungered prayers. But wait… Something's wrong! The metal spring stopped just before your lunch dropped to the bottom of the machine and into your loving arms! It's at that moment you wish you were Reed Richards from the Fantastic Four and you could reach into that machine and take by force that which is rightfully yours. You try to reach in through the bottom of the machine, but you can't lay hold of your item. It is at that moment that your Christian faith is tested. So you look around and if someone happens to be there you say something witty like, "Wow! What are the chances of that Kit Kat getting stuck? Call Ripley." But once that person leaves, you start hitting that machine in a manner that Rocky Balboa didn't even experience in his first fight with Apollo Creed! What's the problem here? The issue is no longer about food. This has now become a matter of principle. You delivered on your end of the bargain; the machine should do so as well. It's only fair. But then again, life isn't fair. You've been hearing that since you were six and someone broke one of your Transformers, but now you're living it.

Life isn't like a vending machine. It's much more complex than that, especially when it involves our relationship with God. Honestly, the name we have for our involvement with God – a relationship, this alone should give it away. We are in a relationship with God, and at what point was a relationship about exactly the equal amount you put into it? Not any healthy relationship I know. Most married couples that end up in my office didn't get there based on unconditional love and sacrificial devotion. They got there because they wanted a vending machine-type of relationship. The problem is, that is not a relationship. That's called a transaction, and God isn't interested in that. But let's be honest, don't we wish at times that we had a transaction-based relationship with God? Don't we wish our connection with God were more like a vending machine and a little less like a personal relationship? Could that be why the best selling Christian books are those that teach us to pray a certain way, so that we can then make God our debtor and we simply have to press a button and whatever we want is waiting for us at the bottom of the machine? It's as simple as putting quarters in a vending machine…or is it? But if you have been a follower of Jesus for any length of time, you probably know by now that God does not operate in that way. He is much too personal to accept that type of arrangement. His plans for us are way too good to let us ruin them by our own shortsightedness and greed.

WE ARE IN A RELATIONSHIP WITH GOD, AND AT WHAT POINT WAS A RELATIONSHIP ABOUT EXACTLY THE EQUAL AMOUNT YOU PUT INTO IT? NOT ANY HEALTHY RELATIONSHIP I KNOW.

John the Baptist is learning this lesson. Yet I would venture to say, this is the hardest lesson he ever had to learn. How would I know this? Probably because this lesson was the hardest for me to learn and I bet the same is true for you. Yet it is only through embracing this life lesson that we will truly start a revolution in our world because it is the one characteristic that will show us who we are consumed by—either God or our own agenda.

THE LESSON IS SIMPLY THIS:
"WHEN I'M CONFRONTED WITH WHAT I DON'T UNDERSTAND, WILL I FALL BACK ON WHAT I DO UNDERSTAND?"

It is a simple statement to say, but it can be as complex as a Rubic's Cube to live out. The reason is because I don't know if we ever really get this principle down. It's not the like riding a bike, where once you learn to do it you never forget. This is the kind of question that pops up every so often in our lives. It appears in different forms and mutates as we get older and hopefully wiser.

THE YOUNG AND THE RESTLESS

But before I get to John's dilemma, let me tell you another story. I'm sure you've watched a soap opera before. If you haven't, you're probably lying. I did. I started watching "Dallas" when I was about eight. I know they call it a "Prime-time drama", but these shows are simply just soap operas at night. Well, you know how complicated the storylines to these shows can be. You can't just start watching in the middle of one episode and know what's going on. Instead, someone you love or who you think loves you usually helps you get sucked into these twisted worlds where two people get married only to find out they are brother and sister. Where a man has a daughter, but because of a document signed by his grandmother, he is now his daughter's niece. The stories are very involved and that's how we keep watching for years. The story I am going to tell you is the equivalent to a biblical soap opera. The story starts with a man named Herod the Great. Herod is the king of Judea, which is a region of Israel. The Roman Empire had conquered most of the known world at that time and Israel was simply a province in their vast territory. Herod was a short, maniacal, paranoid man. This guy was so twisted that he murdered some of his own children and even his beloved wife Miriamne because he was convinced they had a plot to kill him. But after some time he missed the wife whom he killed and erected a statue of her to keep him company. That statue was not the only creation he constructed.

Herod knew that to be remembered as someone great, you had to be one of two types of men: a warrior or a builder. Being the wimp that he was, he chose the latter and began to build. Herod's buildings were some of the greatest buildings known in the ancient world. He spent over 46 years remodeling the holy Temple of Jerusalem.

IN FACT, IT WAS SAID OF THE
JEWISH TEMPLE,
"WHOEVER HAS NOT SEEN
HEROD'S BUILDING - HAS NOT
SEEN A BEAUTIFUL BUILDING
   IN HIS LIFE."

Herod also built the impressive fortress of Masada, and the city of Caesarea, among other astounding buildings including his palace, which was said to have two main buildings, a banquet hall in each, baths, and accommodations for hundreds of guests.[17] Essentially, it was a first century Ritz-Carlton hotel! Yet as gifted as Herod was in construction, he was as villainous in his dealings. It was Herod who killed all the babies in Bethlehem (Matthew 2) because there was only one king of the Jews and that was him! It was Herod who, on his deathbed, detained 10,000 leading Jews that were to be killed the moment he died. Why would someone do such a thing? So when Herod died, it would be remembered as a day of mourning. Herod died, but the order was not carried out and those in custody were set free.

After Herod's death, Caesar allowed the Herod family to remain in power and Israel was divided up amongst the remaining sons of Herod. Philip ruled the northeast area of Israel, which included the cities of Caesarea Philippi and Gamala.[18] Philip had taken a wife named Herodias who also happened to be his niece. But when Herodias saw Philip's lack of desire for power, she left Philip for his brother Antipas. Antipas was given rule over the area of Galilee, which included the cities of Capernaum and Tiberias, as well the region east of the Jordan river called, "Perea" (modern day Jordan), which is referred to in the New Testament as, "Judea across the Jordan." (Matthew 19:1) Due to the fact that John the Baptist spent most of his time in Herod Antipas' jurisdiction, Antipas was certainly aware of John's existence and influence with the people. When Antipas took his brother's wife as his own, John could not keep silent.

> **For Herod had arrested and imprisoned John as a favor to his wife Herodias (the former wife of Herod's brother Philip). John kept telling Herod, "It is illegal for you to marry her." Herod would have executed John, but he was afraid of a riot, because all the people believed John was a prophet.**
> (MATTHEW 14:3-5 NLT)

Scholars suggest that John was in prison for ten months before his death. Yet I can't help but think about what he must have been thinking and expecting during this time. If I put myself in his sandals and in his cell, I know what I would have said if I were John…

Day 1: "Jesus is going to bust me out of here, warden! I'd hate to be you when He shows up. The Messiah turns water into wine and He's on His way. He's going to turn you into matzo ball soup!"

Day 2: "He's on His way by now. Don't bother serving me breakfast, I'll be outta here by lunch time."

Day 3: "Warden, did I ever tell you that the Messiah is my cousin?

Yeah, that's right. He wouldn't leave me hanging. He probably just had to raise the dead and heal some people on His way here. This three-day thing is just for dramatic effect. I think it's going to going to be His trademark!

After a month went by, I'm sure John started to worry. Three months go by and John is in a full-on depression. After six months he starts repenting of things he's never even done, but there has to be a reason why Jesus hasn't shown up. I mean, after all, John always did the right thing and when you do the right thing you always get treated fairly, right? So after ten months, John's disciples visit him and he asks them to deliver Jesus a message…

> **And when John had heard in prison about the works of Christ, he sent two of his disciples and said to Him, "Are You the Coming One, or do we look for another?" Jesus answered and said to them, "Go and tell John the things which you hear and see: The blind see and the lame walk; the lepers are cleansed and the deaf hear; the dead are raised up and the poor have the gospel preached to them. And blessed is he who is not offended because of Me."**
> (MATTHEW 11:2-6 NKJV)

DECIPHERING THE CODE

Have you ever listened to a conversation where you are speaking the same language, but you still don't understand what's being said? That's how I felt recently in a meeting with two architects that are involved in the building my church is constructing. Everything was going along fine when all of a sudden they broke out into an architectural shorthand/dialect that may as well have been Mandarin because I did not understand a word. I picked up on words that sounded like English, but I couldn't be sure. They asked each other about something called, "CAD." I wasn't sure if this was a product they used or if they were insulting me (yes, I've done that with people who don't speak Spanish). I have a tendency to say really dumb things in those kinds of situations. So I asked, "Are those #2 pencils you use? That's my personal preference also. While I'm not an architect, I do know one. His name is Mike Brady. You may know his kids: Greg, Peter, Bobby, Marsha, Jan, and Cindy." That day with the architects is how I felt when I used to read this conversation between Jesus and John. I felt like John and Jesus were speaking in a code that I didn't understand. Everyone else I knew never questioned it, so I figured they understood what it meant. I learned later, they didn't get it either. But what bothered me the most is that it seemed as though Jesus didn't answer John's question. At least that's what I thought until I understood the code they were speaking in.

HERE'S A HINT

Jewish children in biblical times began learning the Torah from age six. Jews believed that the Torah was life, so you would memorize every verse of the Torah by age 10, and by the time you were 15 years old, you had memorized the rest of the Old Testament. So Rabbis, knowing that their students had all of Scripture memorized, would implement a system of teaching called, "Remez." Remez simply means, "A hint."[19] So when a Rabbi was asked a question, he would not just give the answer. Instead, he would pose another question to the student, or he would quote a text from the Bible. But this text would not be the answer to the question either; the verse preceding or succeeding it would give the answer. This was the Rabbis' way of making the students think even while receiving an answer to their question. So if you asked a Rabbi what color the sky was, he could respond, "Well, roses are red." From that you would know that the next "verse"

SO IF YOU ASKED A RABBI WHAT COLOR THE SKY WAS, HE COULD RESPOND, "WELL, ROSES ARE RED."

says, "Violets are blue" and there was your answer. This clears up so much for me when I read the gospels because I would read stories about Jesus talking to the Pharisees and the next verse would say, "And they picked up stones to kill Him." I would feel like a verse was missing in my Bible. But understanding the teaching method of Remez, they knew what Jesus was saying to them, which usually wasn't very flattering and that's why they wanted to kill Him.

RSVP

So what was John asking Jesus and what did Jesus' response mean? John was simply asking, "Are you the Messiah?" Why would he ask that? This was due to a Bible verse that outlined the ministry of the Messiah, so when He arrived people would know how to recognize Him.

> **"The Spirit of the Lord GOD is upon Me, because the LORD has anointed Me to preach good tidings to the poor; He has sent Me to heal the brokenhearted, to proclaim liberty to the captives, and the opening of the prison to those who are bound..."**
>
> (ISAIAH 61:1 NKJV)

So what does the Rabbi Jesus do? He quotes the verse John is thinking of, but He omits the one thing John is looking for. The reason? It is because Jesus is sending John a message—and the message is, "You're going to die in prison." That's why Jesus adds, "Blessed is the person who isn't offended because of Me." Jesus is asking John, "Will you still follow Me even if I don't meet your required expectations?"

Let's be honest, most of us have expectations of God. There are things we want God to do and that is sometimes the motivation to why we choose the right decision over the wrong one. Yet the question that remains is, "What happens when I do the right thing but the wrong result happens?" It is in those moments that I am standing in front of the vending machine again, kicking and punching so I can get my hands on what I paid for. Why? Because it's only fair!

BUT AS A FOLLOWER OF JESUS, WHAT HAPPENS WHEN LIFE ISN'T FAIR OR YOU PERCEIVE GOD AS UNFAIR? WILL YOU STILL FOLLOW JESUS EVEN WHEN THINGS DON'T GO YOUR WAY?

That's an easy question to answer when we are sitting in church or at a small group Bible study, but this is a question every one of us has to answer every day of our lives. No matter where you are in life: young, old, married, or single, we all struggle at times with the vending machine view of God. When you've prayed to be healed of an illness and nothing has happened, will you still follow God? When you've cried out to God because all you want is to have a child, and years have gone by without God answering that prayer, will you still obey Him? You have prayed and fasted for your spouse to change and for your marriage to improve, but God has chosen not to answer yet, will you still follow? When your children decide to rebel and all the rules, discipline, counseling, and prayer has not changed them, will you still follow God? Have you prayed to find that person to spend the rest of your life with, and you are still alone? Will you still follow God, even if He doesn't change things? What do we do in those moments? And trust me, those moments will come. The moments when you pray and you feel as though they hit the ceiling and bounce right back down to earth. The times where nothing seems to go the way you hoped and you say things like, "This wasn't the way I had it all planned out! It was never supposed to be like this!" What will you do in the seasons where you haven't heard from God and it's not because you haven't cried out to Him?

HEARING AID

I am just getting through one of those seasons now where you don't know why things are happening the way they are. It wasn't long ago that I was crying out to God because there were so many decisions to be made and people were expecting answers from me and I had none to give. God was silent and the silence was absolutely deafening. This may sound odd to you, but I had gotten

really used to God speaking to me. Whenever
I had an issue, problem, or decision to make, I
would read the Bible and the answer was always
there, but not during this season. Nothing
seemed to make sense. So I finally broke down
and I asked the question that John asked. I cried
out to God and said, "Are You really who You
say You are?" At that moment, when I reached
the point of utter desperation and I couldn't
turn anywhere else, God broke the silence. So
what did God tell me? Like my friend John the
Baptist, God told me something I didn't want to
hear. It was a verse I had memorized years ago.
It's not the kind of verse you try to memorize,
but it's one that sticks in your mind because
of its potency. I was looking for something
along the lines of Romans 8:38-39 about how
nothing can separate me from the love of God
or Philippians 4:13 where we can do all things
through Christ who gives us strength. Instead,
this verse burst into my mind like Fourth of July
fireworks in front of the backdrop of a midnight
sky. It said, *"Though He slay me, yet will I trust
Him…" (Job 13:15 NKJV).* No promise of change.
No four points to getting out of your slump. It
was just the words of a man, Job, who went
through far worse than I had and was still was
able to say, "I will trust God, no matter what!"
That's the message of Jesus to John the Baptist
in the prison at Machaerus. The message was,
"Will you trust Me no matter what?" At that
moment in my life, I decided I was going to trust
God even if it killed me! I decided that when I
was confronted with what I did not understand,
I was going to fall back on what I do understand.

What I am writing you isn't just theory or
flowery words, it's life…it's my life. And I believe
at some point in your walk with Jesus, it will be

INSTEAD, THIS VERSE BURST INTO MY MIND LIKE FOURTH OF JULY FIREWORKS IN FRONT OF THE BACKDROP OF A MIDNIGHT SKY. IT SAID, "THOUGH HE SLAY ME, YET WILL I TRUST HIM…" (JOB 13:15 NKJV).

your life too. There will be times when you have given your whole life to God and then wondered why He wasn't coming through on His end of the bargain. It's in those moments that you ask if Jesus is who He said He is and if the Christian life is really the best possible way to live. Yet what I have learned in walking through seasons like this is that it reflects back to me who I really believe in. What I learned is that much of the time I do not believe in God, I believe in a transaction-based exchange with God. I believe in the God of the vending machine—the God that gives me what I bargained for when I put enough quarters in the slot. But we must realize that this is not Christianity. This is not what Jesus gave His life for, and this certainly is not what it means to be a follower of His. Being a disciple of Jesus means I say to God, "Do whatever you want with my life. It's OK with me." I do not want to make this seem overly simplistic or easy to do. It's not. Every solid Christian I know has spent every moment of his or her life trying to live out that statement. It will be no different for us. It is here that true trust in God is built in us.

IN THE MOMENT WHERE
I AM
CONFRONTED
WITH SITUATIONS,
PROBLEMS,
AND DIFFICULTIES
THAT I DON'T UNDERSTAND,
I STILL MUST CHOOSE TO
TRUST.
THE DAY I CHOOSE TO ACCEPT
WHATEVER IT IS GOD HAS FOR
ME IS THE DAY I ADD THIS
ELEMENT OF JOHN'S INTO MY
LIFE, AND THE RESULT IS THAT
I CAN START
A REVOLUTION IN MY WORLD.

This begins once I end the revolutionary war inside of me and I wave the white flag and tell God, "You win."

CHAPTER 08

zombies

chapter 08//**zombies**

I was six when I discovered what Halloween was all about. My cousin, Ileana, was going to a Halloween party and she invited me to come along. When we got to the door of the home where the party was happening, I asked if it was okay that I had no costume. Everyone there was decked out in a costume totally appropriate for the times. It was 1979, so there were Darth Vaders, Storm Troopers, Supermans, and someone was even dressed like the devil. That has always been a weird person to pick. No one dresses up like Hitler, so why dress up like Hitler's boss? Well anyway, I was wearing blue jeans and a white shirt. If it was six years later, I could have gone as Bruce Springsteen and sang "Dancing in the Dark" or "Glory Days." But it was 1979 and Abba was blasting through the blown speakers in the house. Due to my costume dilemma, my cousin grabbed some dirt from a potted plant on the front porch and rubbed it all over my shirt. Then she gave personality to this creation of hers. She said, "If anyone asks, tell them you're a zombie." People asked. The problem was nobody thought I was a zombie because they all said I looked too alive. But I couldn't help looking alive. I was alive and still continue to be to this day.

Since that day I have become somewhat of an aficionado when it comes to zombies. I have seen all the required zombie movies: *Return of the Living Dead*, *Day of the Dead*, *Dawn of the Dead*, *Night of the Living Dead*, and of course, *Evil Dead 1, 2, and 3* (subtitled, *Army of Darkness*). So here's what I've realized about zombies: they have the wrong image of themselves. It's true. They still think they're alive, but can't figure out why they want to eat people's brains. So here's a word of warning: if you ever have a craving for a brain on bread sandwich, you may be in trouble.

There's another movie that I really liked growing up. It was called *Weekend at Bernie's*. I remember going to see it with my friends. We would spend our summer vacations going to the movies at the East Side Cinemas in Brockton, Massachusetts where I grew up. We would walk home from the latest movie talking about how we were going to do exactly what we saw on the big screen. I remember seeing the movie *Explorers*. The caption for the film was: "The adventure begins in your own backyard." We were so excited after seeing this movie about three kids that built a spaceship out of parts they found behind their house, that we started scrounging and looking for items to build our own spaceship. We couldn't find any of the stuff they used, so we built a fort instead. But when we saw *Weekend at Bernie's*, we talked about how great it would be to have a dead guy to hang out with. If he was as cool as Bernie, he could pay for stuff and get us into places, and we could reap the rewards as his friends did. But the problem with Bernie is that he's dead. Even when *Weekend at Bernie's 2* was released (I've always wondered why movies like this have sequels – were there any unanswered questions from the first film?), the caption read, "He's back, and he's still dead!" Needless to say, we couldn't find a dead guy to hang out with, so we went back to building our fort.

CHRISTIAN ZOMBIES

I've learned something about observing people as a Christian. Most people are going through life in a zombie-like state. It's like there's a new Bernie in town! There's a great deal of people who are dead, yet they walk around like they're alive. I'm not talking about non-Christians that haven't experienced the life-giving message of the Gospel. I'm talking about Christians who are under a delusion as to what life is exactly.

HERE IS HOW IT WORKS FOR MANY PEOPLE: A FEW TIMES IN LIFE WE MEET SOMEONE WHO'S REALLY ALIVE.

The kind of person we wish we could be more like. They are passionate, daring, adventurous, focused, and consumed by something or someone. We look at those people as the exception rather than the rule. We label these people as anomalies that don't factor into the equation of what life is. Yet what I've learned is that "alive" is the perfect description of John the Baptist. He was courageous, zealous, outspoken, purposed, and radical about what he believed. God consumed him and it drew people to him because that is what life does by nature. It draws us in like a mosquito to a blue, glowing light. Life is constantly calling us to join it. The morning sun calls to us to experience the glory of the day. The evening breeze tempts us to embrace its richness and unwind from a day of labor. At the same time, a life that is lived for God's glory calls us out of the shadows of mediocrity and demands our participation. It gently requests our presence and at the same time pokes us like a spur to move into its light. We live under the impression that life is what we get when we first draw breath. Our first breath gave us existence, but only God can give us life. So as I watch humanity makes its choices and set its priorities, I have noted something that needs to be understood if we are going to understand John the Baptist's death. It is that everyone dies, but not everyone really lives.

THE ODD COUPLE

I believe that's why John was put next to another man at the end of his life. I find that the Bible does this all the time. Maybe it's because God likes to show us the contrasts. Maybe it's because there are so few great people in this world that everyone seems to pale in comparison to the men the Bible zeroes in on. But King David was put next to King Saul to show David's heart for God over Saul's selfish heart. Jesus and Pilate share center stage for a

LIFE IS CONSTANTLY CALLING US TO JOIN IT. THE MORNING SUN CALLS TO US TO EXPERIENCE THE GLORY OF THE DAY.

brief moment to show us what true power and true submission are. But the man John was positioned next to was juxtaposed to him in every way by every standard. Yet, if we were honest, most of us would choose to be him over John the Baptist if we didn't know the story. This man wasn't half the man John was and he never started a revolution in his world even though he had wealth, power, and fame at his disposal. He lacked the elements that John had. The reason he lacked them is because this man was a zombie. He was Bernie. He was dead and he didn't even know it. He walked through life existing and never embraced the life God dreamed for him to take hold of—the same life God dreams for us to take hold of.

> At that time Herod the tetrarch heard the reports about Jesus, and he said to his attendants, "This is John the Baptist; he has risen from the dead! That is why miraculous powers are at work in him." Now Herod had arrested John and bound him and put him in prison because of Herodias, his brother Philip's wife, for John had been saying to him: "It is not lawful for you to have her." Herod wanted to kill John, but he was afraid of the people, because they considered him a prophet. On Herod's birthday the daughter of Herodias danced for them and pleased Herod so much that he promised with an oath to give her whatever she asked. Prompted by her mother, she said, "Give me here on a platter the head of John the Baptist." The king was distressed, but because of his oaths and his dinner guests, he ordered that her request be granted and had John beheaded in the prison. His head was brought in on a platter and given to the girl, who carried it to her mother. John's disciples came and took his body and buried it. Then they went and told Jesus. When Jesus heard what had happened, he withdrew by boat privately to a solitary place...

(MATTHEW 14:1-13 NIV)

I will be the first one to admit to you that I like Hollywood endings. I believe there are two basic rules all films must follow no matter what genre they are.

RULE #1 – YOU CANNOT, UNDER ANY CIRCUMSTANCES, DESTROY THE EARTH.

Many movies don't have a problem with this rule, but Science Fiction can get a little out of control at times. So I state this rule because humans should always have a home. That is why *Beneath the Planet of the Apes* has an unacceptable ending. Destroying the earth is never an option! Let's just agree on it and life as we know it will be better.

RULE #2 – YOU CANNOT, UNDER ANY CIRCUMSTANCES, KILL THE MAIN CHARACTER.

People are getting a little loose with this rule, and more and more movies are doing this for shock value. Human beings love happy endings. I go to the movies because I want to escape from real life. So when someone puts out a movie that is just like real life, I am not interested. If I want real life, I'll open my window or turn on the news. But I go to the movies because they take me to a place where good guys always win and bad guys always get what's coming to them. So I get angry when movies don't turn out the way I had hoped. I love the movie *Gladiator*. It is a brilliant film. I saw it in the theatre and fell in love with the story. So when the film was released on DVD, I bought it. But to this day I have never watched it. The DVD could be blank for all I know. Why have I never watched the DVD? It's because the ending doesn't meet my standards of happy endings. It violates the second rule and I can't deal with that. Think about the ending to *Gladiator* for a moment. What is the only thing that Maximus wants? To be reunited with his family. So he dies at the end of the film and he says, "I'm going home." The scene shows his family waiting for him in some version of heaven that Hollywood created. So what's wrong with that? Here's my problem: Maximus kills Commodus and I am hoping that Maximus will become emperor of Rome. Isn't that just poetic justice? What I have begun to realize is that to Maximus, like John the Baptist, it wasn't about the glory on earth. It was about eternal glory that was waiting for him.

DIRTY DANCING

There's something for us to learn here in this death scene with John. While it seems like the ultimate bad ending, it's not. Now let me say, I didn't always think that. I mean I understood that John died. I could deal with that. But it was the way John died that I couldn't accept. I can handle Jack dying at the end of *Titanic* to save Rose's life. It violates the second rule, but rules can be bent now and again. But John wasn't saving a life, or preaching a message, or defending the helpless. He was the payment for a dance on some idiot's birthday! Please don't think that just because the dance mentioned is in the Bible that we're talking about the Macarena or the Electric Slide. This was dirty dancing. It was perverse and base—an old man getting his kicks watching his stepdaughter dance for him. To make matters worse, Herod decided to honor the girl's request to kill John. I am outraged! We hear about scenes like this from time to time and we ask, "Why? How could this happen?" We lament over someone who dies younger than normal, but that's not the question we should be asking ourselves. We should be thinking, "How do people die without ever living?" How is it that this world is filled with Christian zombies who aren't alive because they have never taken up the life God offers? In his book, _The Barbarian Way_, Erwin McManus explains this point by sharing the following: "Somewhere along the way the movement of Jesus Christ became civilized as Christianity. We created a religion using the name of Jesus Christ and convinced ourselves that God's optimal desire for our lives was to insulate us in a spiritual bubble where we risk nothing, sacrifice nothing, lose nothing, worry about nothing. Yet Jesus' death wasn't to free us from dying, but to free us from the fear of death. Jesus came to liberate us so that we could die up front and then live…Rather than living a long life, are you willing to live a life worth living?"[20] Jesus put it this way…

> **If you try to keep your life for yourself, you will lose it. But if you give up your life for me, you will find true life.**
> (MATTHEW 16:25 NLT)

Newsflash: this is the Christian life! Some people are under the impression that believing in Jesus intellectually creates this invisible barrier that only good things can pass through. We're just rowing our boats gently down the stream, and merrily, merrily, merrily, merrily, life is but a dream. If that's what we think, then it's time for the alarm to go off because we need to wake up! To be consumed by God means that you will lose your life, either literally or by denying yourself daily and taking up your cross. We have a hard time identifying with John because we haven't discovered that death is part of the Christian life. That's why many of our lives reflect Herod's existence over John's life. It is like the movie _Braveheart_. We so desperately want to be William Wallace but we end up being Robert the Bruce instead. The reason is no one wants to be the guy who gets his head chopped off, no matter how great he is! It's the same reason I hear when I talk to people who have given up on Jesus. When I inquire as to why, they say some variation of how Jesus did not come through for them. So I normally ask them, "What did He promise?" They reply, "Well, He didn't help me in my situation." So I say, "But you didn't answer my question. What did He promise?" Silence usually follows. Then I share what Jesus promised to every person who decided to be His disciple:

I have told you all this so that you may have peace in me. Here on earth you will have many trials and sorrows. But take heart, because I have overcome the world.
(JOHN 16:33 NLT)

A FORWARDING ADDRESS

That's what Jesus promised to His disciples. Yet most of us get upset with God because we have a different view of life on earth than He does. We tend to get heaven and earth confused. The life without any problems, aches, and pains doesn't have an earthly address. That's heaven. Many people are Herod in disguise because we want our version of heaven while we're still here on earth. Personally, I don't think that heaven is going to be anything like what we expect. We aren't going to be sitting on clouds playing harps nor singing songs forever and ever. It is also not going to be like the cover of 1984 by Van Halen with an angel smoking a cigarette. What will it be? We don't really know. We know Jesus is preparing the place for us. I see huge books on the subject of heaven. I always wonder what their authors write about because the Bible doesn't tell us much about heaven. We only get some brief characteristics here and there. I wish Paul would have told us about what he saw when he was there. All we are told of his visit is…

…Let me tell about the visions and revelations I received from the Lord. I was caught up into the third heaven fourteen years ago. Whether my body was there or just my spirit, I don't know; only God knows. But I do know that I was caught up into paradise and heard things so astounding that they cannot be told.
(2 CORINTHIANS 12:1-4 NLT)

Paul is just like a friend that doesn't send you a postcard when he or she goes on vacation. He visits a great place, but doesn't spill the beans. Here's what I have decided: God is keeping it a secret because He wants to surprise us. So whatever notion we have about heaven is probably way off course from the real thing. Yet our expectations here on earth are what get us into trouble. The Christian life is not about getting heaven into our lives; it's about getting people into heaven.

When we decide to be Herod in the story and not John, we only delay the inevitable. It may come as a shock to you, but Herod Antipas is no longer with us. He died not that long after John. The difference was John was really alive and Herod was just a zombie. What I find fascinating is what happened to Herod after John's death. The father of his first wife, whom he left for Herodias, was the king of the Nabataeans. He came against Herod and defeated him in battle. Amazingly, the Jews believed that this was divine punishment for what he did to John. The Jewish historian Josephus wrote, *"Now, some of the Jews thought that the destruction of Herod's army came from God, and that very justly, as a punishment of what he did against John, that was called the Baptist; for Herod slew him, who was a good man, and commanded the Jews to exercise virtue, both as to righteousness toward one another, and piety towards God, and so to come to baptism... Now the Jews had an opinion that the destruction of this army was sent as a punishment upon Herod, and a mark of God's displeasure against him." (Antiquities 16:5:2).*[21] Soon after this, Herod's nephew, Agrippa, convinced the Roman Emperor, Caligula, to give Antipas' title, wealth, and kingdom to him. Antipas' very own nephew stole all he had! Then, Antipas was exiled to Gaul where he died. What a pathetic story. After all of his striving, Antipas ended up with nothing but a sad legacy. Yet it's the story of many people. I gave the commencement

THE CHRISTIAN LIFE IS NOT ABOUT GETTING HEAVEN INTO OUR LIVES; IT'S ABOUT GETTING PEOPLE INTO HEAVEN.

speech at a graduation recently and I talked to the students about John the Baptist. I told them that what will make all the difference between living and existing is how much they open themselves up to God's plan for their lives. Herod Antipas chose to simply exist and he is just a footnote in history. John chose to live life God's way. The result is that when we think of the gospels, we can't tell the story of Jesus without telling John's story.

About four years ago, a guy that I knew died. He and I weren't friends, but I knew who he was. He had left America to be a missionary and start a church. The church was doing very well and he was the pastor. From what I knew of him, he was a radical guy. He was full of life, enthusiasm, and passion for Jesus. One day, he and a friend had gone surfing for the morning and he drowned. Just like that, he was gone. There were no warnings, and no time for preparation. When I was told the news, I got the same feelings that I had when I first read this passage about John's death—I was overwhelmed. You see, I lived in a dream world. I thought I was in a spiritual bubble. I thought that pastors were immune from this sort of tragedy. I believed that God would protect pastors in a special way and keep us from harm by nature of our calling. So this news rocked my world because for the first time in my life I felt exposed. I felt as though if someone wanted to get to me, they could. I attended his memorial service even though he and I didn't know each other, and I sat in the back row as over 500 people showed up to celebrate his life and tell stories of what he meant to each of them. I have to be honest; the only person on my mind that morning was me. I couldn't believe that God would allow a missionary pastor to die what I thought was a meaningless death. "A surfing accident is no way for a pastor to die," I thought silently.

THEN I REMEMBERED JOHN THE BAPTIST AS I LOOKED OVER THE CROWD OF MISSIONARIES, PASTORS, LEADERS, FAMILY, AND FRIENDS THAT WERE PRESENT.

Like John, this man had touched many lives; I had no right to think of his death as meaningless. His death was meaningful because his life was meaningful. Not very many people are able to say that they lived the life that this man lived. In fact, most people aren't able to say they have ever lived at all. Most people die long before the funeral, just like Herod. In contrast, John the Baptist didn't ever have to spend a moment of his life wondering if what he was doing was making a difference. He is the model to all of humanity as to how to really live and start a revolution in the world. John paved the way. But that shouldn't surprise us, because that's what a snowplow does...

CHAPTER 09

wet cement

chapter 09//wet cement

In 1995 when I was on tour with my band, we had a couple of shows and a video shoot in California. We decided to take an afternoon and go to Hollywood. I love movies, so the thought of going to Tinsel Town has always excited me. I wanted to see Hollywood for one reason: Mann's Chinese Theatre! Every major movie premiere is there and lots of famous people have their handprints in the cement as you enter the property. The day I went there I had only one object of interest—the imprints made by the cast of the original *Star Trek*. When they signed the wet cement and put their handprints in the ground, they forever marked their places of influence on the television and motion picture industry.

WHEN I SAW THE PRINTS,
I THREW MYSELF TO THE
GROUND AND LAY NEXT TO
THEM.

I asked a friend to take a picture, which I still have to this day. It must be amazing to have left such an impression in your field that you are asked to physically leave one as well.

As I was thinking about that summer day in 1995, I thought back to the day I left an impression on wet cement. I was living in Brockton, Massachusetts and I was watching a house being built right around the corner from my own home. I had a quarter in my pocket and when the builders laid the foundation and left for the day, I took out a quarter and wrote, "Robert Franquiz was here!" Then I put my quarter next to it. My plan was simple. I thought that if I put a quarter there, years down the line I would be able to come back and tell the homeowners I wanted my quarter back, and they would have to dig up the floor. Because they would be unwilling to dig up the floor, I would ask for $25 as payoff for not taking legal action! Yes, I must admit, even at age ten, I was a genius!

EVERYONE IS IMPRESSIVE

What I've learned since that summer day from my childhood is this: It's not some people who leave an impression, everyone does. We call it a legacy. It is simply the impression that you and I have made in the people who are around us. I used to have this belief that only rich, famous, or important people left legacies. Instead, what I have noted is that everyone leaves a legacy. We simply decide whether it will be a good or bad one. When you think of a legacy, if you're anything like me, you think of an inheritance left to children, or as a discovery someone makes that changes life as we know it, but I believe it is something far simpler and much more important than those scenarios. I believe your legacy is the difference you leave behind, not the stuff your leave behind. It's why I have changed how I ask kids what they plan on doing with their lives. I used to ask, "What are you going to be when you grow up?" But now I ask them, "How are you going to make the world a better place? How are you going to change the world?" Because then the focus is not on WHAT they are going to be when they reach adulthood. The focus is on WHO they are going to be starting right now! John the Baptist's legacy is what solidified him as the greatest man ever. He was anything but a "flash in the pan" preacher that no one remembered after he was gone. Instead, you cannot tell the story of Jesus without talking about John the Baptist first. All four gospels start with the story of John who paved the way. That's when it struck me that your legacy isn't the stuff you leave behind; it's the difference you leave behind. Jesus said:

> I assure you, of all who have ever lived, none is greater than John the Baptist. Yet even the most insignificant person in the Kingdom of Heaven is greater than he is! And from the time John the Baptist began preaching and baptizing until now, the Kingdom of Heaven has been

> forcefully advancing, and violent people attack
> it. For before John came, all the teachings of the
> Scriptures looked forward to this present time.
> And if you are willing to accept what I say, he is
> Elijah, the one the prophets said would come·
> Anyone who is willing to hear should listen and
> understand!
> (MATTHEW 11:11-15 NLT)

I am always blown away by this passage because Jesus is linking
the beginning of the kingdom with the ministry of John the Baptist.
That's why he said since John started preaching, the kingdom had
been advancing. Imagine that being your legacy—the guy who
kicked off the Gospel age! The people listening to Jesus would have
understood this. The Messianic expectation in Israel was at an all-
time high! So the country was waiting for the man to show up who
would pave the way for the Messiah's coming. That is why Jesus
linked John to Elijah. The people were well aware of God's promise
to send Elijah before the coming of the Lord.

> Look, I am sending you the prophet Elijah before
> the great and dreadful day of the LORD arrives.
> His preaching will turn the hearts of parents to
> their children, and the hearts of children to their
> parents...
> (MALACHI 4:5-6 NLT)

When we compare that promise with Luke's recording of the
conversation between the angel Gabriel and Zechariah, the father of
John the Baptist, the pieces begin to fit.

> And he will persuade many Israelites to turn
> to the Lord their God. He will be a man with
> the spirit and power of Elijah, the prophet of
> old. He will precede the coming of the Lord,
> preparing the people for his arrival. He will turn
> the hearts of the fathers to their children, and he
> will change disobedient minds to accept godly
> wisdom.
> (LUKE 1:16-17 NLT)

Think of that legacy! Turning the hearts of fathers back to their kids and bringing peace in homes where chaos once ruled. We tend to think of legacy as something that we leave at the end of our lives. Yet I hope you are beginning to entertain the thought that it might be something else entirely. Our legacy is what we do with the sum of our lives and the difference we make with our lives. Dads, what is the impression you're making on the lives of your kids? Are you teaching them to walk with God by your example, or are you hoping they will do the right thing even though they haven't seen you do it? Mom, do those kids see a loving relationship between their parents? Whether we want to admit it or not, the kind of relationship we have will be the standard they use in looking for "Mr. or Miss Right." It reminds me of a scene from an episode of the Fox series, "That 70's Show." In this episode, Red (the dad) doesn't want to go to church because he and God are "OK." Kitty (the mom) decides to play along, but the moment the kids use dad not going to church as an excuse as to why they don't want to go, everyone, including dad, is coming to church. Well, you don't even need me to tell you the end of the story. The very next Sunday, the kids don't want to go to church and they ask, "If dad doesn't have to go to church, why do we?" At that moment, Kitty smiles, points at Red and says, "Aha! That's it! Let's all get dressed because the Forman's are going to church!" Red Forman is the average dad in America. He wants his kids to do the right thing, but he just won't go as far as to do it or model it himself. What we tend not to realize is that it is our words followed by actions that leave the impression, not just the words

ARE YOU TEACHING THEM TO WALK WITH GOD BY YOUR EXAMPLE, OR ARE YOU HOPING THEY WILL DO THE RIGHT THING EVEN THOUGH THEY HAVEN'T SEEN YOU DO IT?

themselves. If we want our kids to read the Bible and pray, to trust God daily, and obey God's commands, then guess what? We have to live a life that models it. That's what John did and that's why he started a revolution in his world.

GREAT IMPRESSIONISTS

Mom and Dad, you are leaving your name on the wet cement of your kids' lives. You are leaving your name on the wet cement of your friends and family's lives. Because not only are kids wet cement, here's a little known secret: everyone is wet cement.

YOU AND I HAVE THE ABILITY TO LEAVE A MARK ON ANYONE IN THIS LIFE.

Think of the people who have shaped your thinking and helped you formulate a worldview. These were not just your parents. They were teachers, friends, movies, books, employers, and employees. Some of the people who left their mark on our wet cement were people who were close to us, others were people we have never met, but their works have influenced us.

BUT THE MOST IMPORTANT THING TO REMEMBER IS THAT YOU AND I GET TO CHOOSE WHAT KIND OF LEGACY WE WILL LEAVE.

If we had a choice, most of us would love to be remembered like Alfred Nobel, founder of the Nobel Peace Prize and champion for the cause of peace over Thomas Crapper, inventor of the toilet. You see, while most of us would readily choose Nobel, his legacy did not start in the way it ended. When Alfred's brother died, a local newspaper mistakenly ran an obituary for Alfred instead. The obituary stated that he was known for creating the most destructive force known to mankind—dynamite. When Alfred read it, he decided he did not want to be remembered for destruction, but for peace. So he decided to take his resources and use them for promoting peace. So even though Alfred Nobel invented dynamite, no one remembers him for that, and some when they hear this story are reluctant to believe it at first. The reason is because destruction is not his legacy. Today, when you think of Alfred Nobel, you think of peace because one day he decided that was what he wanted his legacy to be. The difference you make, the mark you leave in the lives of people is your legacy; not the stuff you leave behind.

ONCE UPON A TIME...

Everyday, you and I are in the process of writing our legacies: our actions and words are the pen and history is the paper that we script on. Depending on where we are in our lives, some are putting the finishing touches on their legacy. Others are barely out of the first chapter. The legacy is what those who are influenced by us look like and act like because of our influence in their lives. I, personally, am not looking to some building as my legacy as a pastor. I see those that bear my last name and the lives that I have invested in as my legacy. What about you? In the same way, there are people who have made life-altering decisions because of your example, counsel, and experiences. Those people are wet cement that you have imprinted with your life. The Apostle Paul understood this fact when he wrote the following words...

> **But the only letter of recommendation we need is you yourselves! Your lives are a letter written in our hearts, and everyone can read it and recognize our good work among you.**
> (2 CORINTHIANS 3:2 NLT)

You have an opportunity to start a revolution in your world, if you choose to. You might say, "I'm not the revolutionary type." You're wrong! Everyone is the revolutionary type because we all have the ability to revolutionize a life! Jesus' disciples couldn't share the Gospel without mentioning John's name because the Gospel began with John's ministry.

> **Here begins the Good News about Jesus the Messiah, the Son of God. In the book of the prophet Isaiah, God said, "Look, I am sending my messenger before you, and he will prepare your**

way. He is a voice shouting in the wilderness: 'Prepare a pathway for the Lord's coming! Make a straight road for him!'" This messenger was John the Baptist. He lived in the wilderness and was preaching that people should be baptized to show that they had turned from their sins and turned to God to be forgiven.

(MARK 1:1-4 NLT)

I'M IMPRESSED!

It is impossible for me to share the Gospel without talking about my brother first because before I get to the day I gave my life to Jesus it starts with the one who shared the message of Jesus with me. There are people who can't talk about their relationship with Jesus without mentioning me. I am grateful and humbled by that. Here is what I know as well: there is at least one person whose Gospel story begins with you. It may be your child, a friend, a coworker, or a stranger you met by chance, but somewhere there's a story about Jesus changing a life that begins with you. That's called a legacy. That's called leaving an impression on wet cement. If you have children in your home that don't know Jesus personally, share and model God's love to them. Teach them what it means to walk with God in this world. From the day they are born, until the day they leave for college, you only have 6,570 days. My prayer is that you use them wisely. Once that buzzer sounds and you are out of time, everyone else becomes an influence and begins to make their mark on their lives and

IT MAY BE YOUR CHILD, A FRIEND, A COWORKER, OR A STRANGER YOU MET BY CHANCE, BUT SOMEWHERE THERE'S A STORY ABOUT JESUS CHANGING A LIFE THAT BEGINS WITH YOU. THAT'S CALLED A LEGACY.

leave impressions, and at that point many of us can only watch from the sidelines.

When I was growing up in Boston, some mornings we would wake up and find over a foot of snow on the ground. My step-dad would wake me up and we would get dressed to begin shoveling before we were blocked in because of all the snowfall. He would lead the way and leave impressions in the snow to where we were going to begin shoveling. As I was behind him, what would I do? I would walk where he had already made the impressions and follow in his footsteps. Who we are today is a reflection of those that have written their names in our wet cement.

YET GOD HAS GIVEN US THE
   OPPORTUNITY AND ABILITY
TO INFLUENCE SOMEONE ELSE
FOR THE GOSPEL'S SAKE.

A mom or dad that teaches their children to desire to know God is a person that is writing his or her legacy on the wet cement of a young life—that is your legacy—you are simply creating a path for others to follow.

DR. MCCOY'S IMPRESSION TELLS A TALE

When I was at Mann's Chinese Theatre that day in 1995, I saw something very strange. When I looked at the cement where the cast of the original *Star Trek* series had written their names, I expected William Shatner's (Captain Kirk) name to be the biggest. Yet it wasn't. It was DeForest Kelley's (Dr. McCoy) name that was the largest and most prominent. It didn't make sense to me and I pondered this anomaly for quite some time. I thought the biggest impression should be the most important person, but it wasn't in this case. Then I realized that this is the picture of many lives. There are lesser characters making bigger impressions than the most important people are. What I learned on the floor of the theatre is that in the wet cement of our lives, someone will have the loudest voice and leave the largest mark. It can be the voices that are leading us to step out in faith and trust God with every day He has given to us. Or it can be a lesser voice, a secondary character, that gets top billing and it leads us down another path that we regret.

We can be the loud voice in the lives of others. We can be a voice calling out to others, a handprint pointing the way to the Messiah. If you decide that you desire to leave the kind of impression that John the Baptist left, the kind that marks the beginning of a season of God's grace and redemption, then you have decided to be a person that God can use to touch the lives of others forever. The time of the Gospel began with John's life and example, and people have been pressing into it ever since. Your life's legacy and mine can be the same. The God-stories of countless individuals can begin with our mark, our impression, our example…

epilogue

"I can't get involved! I've got work to do! It's not that I like the Empire. I hate it! But there's nothing I can do about it right now. It's such a long way from here."
- Luke Skywalker

When I watch *Star Wars*, I can't help but look at the story from a bird's eye perspective and think to myself, "Luke, there are important things that need to be done. A Death Star needs to be destroyed! A princess needs to be saved! A rebellion needs to be led! A revolution needs to be started!" Yet most of us, like Luke, can't see the big picture. We can't imagine all that God wants to do in this world. So we relegate ourselves to living out a safe, boring, and mediocre existence instead of embracing the adventure God has planned for each of us. I have always wanted to be Luke Skywalker in the story of my life, but I'm ashamed to admit that all too often I have been C-3PO, looking for the path that is out of harm's way. But I've lived long enough to know that heroes aren't forged on the road to Anchorhead or Mos Eisley. They are made in the trenches trying to destroy the Death Star with one perfect shot, battling a ruthless villain on the cloud city of Besbin, and fighting for good in the forest of Endor. But we tend to live on the outer rim on Tatooine, where nothing can hurt us and where, subsequently, we can never make a difference.

When I started this walk with John the Baptist's life story, I never thought it would change me as much as it did. From the first day, he made me wrestle with the word "revolution." So here's what I have decided: I love the word "revolution!" Do evils start revolutions? Yes they do. But I have recognized that while revolution has two definitions, they can only do the first one. They can only make the merry-go-round motion of moving in circles because throughout history, evil men have been circling Satan's schemes and never getting anywhere further than God has allowed. But great men and women, who love and serve God, have the ability to truly be revolutionary. They can cause sudden, radical, and complete change in this world by partnering with God, and by stepping outside of their comfort zones to live life for the glory of God. They are truly revolutionaries; I pray that one day my life could be numbered with theirs.

My prayer is that walking with John the Baptist has riveted your heart, expanded you mind, and sent your spirit into the place where true heroes are born—the very heart of God. John the Baptist was the greatest man ever. He was truly a revolutionary person that forever left his impression on this planet. This world would never have been the same if not for John, but I ask you to consider this: God did not choose him to live in this age, at this moment in history: God chose you! God is in the midst of starting a revolution and He is looking for men and women who are willing to enlist. People who are willing to give all of themselves because our Savior Jesus gave all of Himself for us. I believe that God has placed you in your world, in your country, in your state, in your city, and in your community because you are part of God's strategic plan to reach the nations with the everlasting Gospel of Jesus. There's a world that's looking for great men and great women who will live the elements that John the Baptist possessed and be the modern day forerunners of the Messiah, Who is soon coming again…

bibliography

(Endnotes)
Introduction: Revolution Calling

[1] Dave Stone, *Refining Your Style* (Group Publishing: Loveland, CO 2004) Pg. 74

Chapter 1: The Greatest Show on Earth

[2] *The New Lexicon Webster's Dictionary* (Lexicon Publications: New York, NY 1988) Pg. 852

[3] *The New Lexicon Webster's Dictionary* (Lexicon Publications: New York, NY 1988) Pg. 852

Chapter 2: Grand-Parents

[4] Rick Warren *The Purpose Driven Life* (Zondervan Publishers: Grand Rapids, MI 2002) Pg. 17

[5] Ray VanderLaan *The People in Jesus' Day: Essenes* (Follow the Rabbi Ministries: Grand Rapids, MI Audio Mp3)

Chapter 3: Born to be Wild

[6] John Eldredge *Wild at Heart* (Thomas Nelson Publishers: Nashville, TN 2001) Pg. 7

Chapter 4: Snowplow

[7] Rick Warren *The Purpose Driven Life* (Zondervan Publishers: Grand Rapids, MI 2002) Pg. 17-18

[8] John Eldredge *Epic* (Thomas Nelson Publishers: Nashville, TN 2004) Pg. 21

[9] Ray VanderLaan *The People in Jesus' Day: Sadducees* (Follow the Rabbi Ministries: Grand Rapids, MI Audio Mp3)

Chapter 5: Floor Model

[10] *The New American Bible* (Catholic Bible Press: Nashville, TN 1991) Pg. 473

[11] *The New American Bible* (Catholic Bible Press: Nashville, TN 1991) Pg. 506-507

[12] *Holman Bible Dictionary* (Holman Bible Publishers: Nashville, TN 1991) Pg. 791

[13] *Holman Bible Dictionary* (Holman Bible Publishers: Nashville, TN 1991) Pg. 298

Chapter 6: Watermark

[xiv] David Stern *Jewish New Testament Commentary* (Jewish New Testament Publications: Clarksville, MD 1989) Pg. 15

[14] Spiros Zodhiates *The Complete Word Study New Testament Dictionary* (AMG International: Chattanooga, TN 1992) Pg. 309

[15] Spiros Zodhiates *The Complete Word Study New Testament Dictionary* (AMG International: Chattanooga, TN 1992) Pg. 1260

Chapter 7: Vending Machine

[16] *Holman Bible Dictionary* (Holman Bible Publishers: Nashville, TN 1991) Pg. 640

[17] *Holman Bible Handbook* (Holman Bible Publishers: Nashville, TN 1992) Pg. 556

[18] David Stern *Jewish New Testament Commentary* (Jewish New Testament Publications: Clarksville, MD 1989) Pg. 61

Chapter 8: Zombies

[19] Erwin Rafael McManus, *The Barbarian Way* (Thomas Nelson Publishers: Nashville, TN 2005) Pg. 49

[20] William Winston *The Works of Josephus* (Hendrickson Publishers: Peabody, MA 1987) Pg. 435

CPSIA information can be obtained
at www.ICGtesting.com
Printed in the USA
FSHW010346051019
62635FS